WELFARE TO WORK
HANDBOOK

EDITED BY **ILSE MOGENSEN**

WELFARE TO WORK HANDBOOK

About this book

The Welfare to Work Handbook draws on *Inclusion's* expertise in benefits and welfare to work programmes to provide a reference guide for anyone involved in the welfare to work agenda or seeking information on the financial support and provisions currently available to those moving towards work.

This handbook is aimed at adults of working age. For specific information on those aged 16-17, *Inclusion* also publishes the **Young Person's Handbook.**

Inclusion also produces **Working in the UK: Newcomer's Handbook, The Young Person's Handbook** and the **Guide for Working Families Handbook.** For information on any of these, please visit our website at **www.cesi.org.uk.**

Acknowledgements

We are grateful for the contributions of the following people in producing this handbook:

Neil Bateman for expertise in welfare rights and social policy
Peter Turville for advising on JSA and studying
Ann Watt for editing the text of the handbook
Caroline Wilding for providing the index
Andy Mattock at origin8 creative for work on design and layout
Simon Ennals, solicitor of Essential Rights for proof-reading the benefits section

Current *Inclusion* staff:
Paul Bivand for expertise on welfare to work programmes
Laurence Bell for research on welfare to work programmes
Justine Roberts and **Rosanna Singler** for research and fact-checking
Becky Shah for proofing and correcting.

Thanks is also due to former *Inclusion* employees **Will Somerville, Chris Brace** and **Bee Brooke,** who contributed to previous publications of which parts have been incorporated into this handbook.

Contents

Part 2: Welfare to work programmes

Contents

1 Introduction to welfare benefits

This part of the book is an introductory level guide to the main benefits which are available to people. Some benefits are paid if you are out of work, others if you meet certain conditions (for example if you have a child) and some also have a means test which looks at your personal circumstances, income and capital.

Most social security benefits are administered by the Department for Work and Pensions (DWP) through three separate services – Jobcentre Plus, the Pensions Service and the Disability and Carers Service. Two benefits are administered by local authorities (LAs) – these are Housing Benefit and Council Tax Benefit – while Child Benefit, Child Tax Credit and Working Tax Credit are administered by Her Majesty's Revenue and Customs (HMRC) (formerly known as the Inland Revenue). Each benefit and tax credit has its own rules of entitlement.

The information in this section gives a general overview of entitlement. It is a complex subject and there are many exceptions to rules, and your circumstances may not fit the rules precisely. It is therefore important to obtain advice from a reputable, independent advice agency.

If you are receiving benefits because you are not in work and you are thinking of taking up a job, it is very important to obtain advice about what the effect of this will be on your overall finances – sometimes, people can find that a job does not pay enough, especially if you have high housing or childcare costs or if the costs of taking a job (such as travel) are high. You can ask a reputable advice agency or the Jobcentre to calculate how your benefits will be affected by taking a particular job, but to calculate this accurately, the adviser will need to know:

- the hourly rate of pay for the job and the number of hours you will be working
- the expenses associated with taking the job (for example, travel to work, work-related clothing and equipment and childcare costs)
- accurate figures for your housing costs
- precise figures for any other income and savings
- your household composition.

If you are a newcomer to the United Kingdom (UK), you may find that you are refused benefits because you need permission from the Home Office Immigration and Nationality Directorate to be in the United Kingdom (you are a 'Person Subject to Immigration Control') or because, even if you are allowed to enter and remain in the UK, benefit officials do not accept that you have a 'right to reside' in the UK or you are not 'habitually resident' and your benefit claim has been refused. There is a right to appeal to an independent Tribunal if you are refused a benefit and you should get help from an independent advice agency if this happens to you. Appeals have a good chance of success, especially if you have someone to represent you.

If you are subject to immigration control and as part of your permission to stay in the United Kingdom you are not allowed to claim 'public funds', you must get independent advice before even enquiring about your benefits at a social security or local authority office. For more details, see The Newcomer's Handbook, published by *Inclusion*.

Outline of the benefits system

The UK's social security benefits system is a mix of different types of benefits each with different rules. There are contributory benefits where entitlement is based on National Insurance records, non-contributory benefits with entitlement based on meeting certain rules of eligibility (neither your income, capital nor your National Insurance record matters, though sometimes your earnings can affect these) and also means-tested benefits with entitlement based on detailed eligibility criteria and rules about income and capital. There are also benefits for employees which are administered by employers (i.e. Statutory Sick Pay and Statutory Maternity, Paternity and Adoption Pay).

Tax Credits are a form of income maintenance based on a mix of social security and income tax rules and are paid by Her Majesty's Revenue and Customs (HMRC).

Finally, there is a range of education benefits administered by the government's Department for Education and Skills and local authorities, and health benefits which can help towards the cost of certain health related costs such as prescriptions. These are administered by the National Health Service. In Wales, Scotland and Northern Ireland, the administrative arrangements for these are slightly different.

Some benefits are designed to fit with others, so it is best to view the social security system as a jigsaw with interlocking pieces because entitlement to one benefit can sometimes be based on entitlement to another benefit. This is done so that particular groups can receive additional help – for example, people with children or people with a disability – and is commonly referred to as 'passporting'.

Benefits at a glance

Contributory benefits	Non-contributory benefits	Means-tested benefits and tax credits	Employee benefits
Retirement Pension ✢ ✦ †	Disability Living Allowance	Income Support	Statutory Sick Pay ▲
Incapacity Benefit ✢ ✦ †	Attendance Allowance	Jobseeker's Allowance ✢	Statutory Maternity Pay ▲
Jobseeker's Allowance ✢ †	Child Benefit	State Pension Credit	Statutory Paternity Pay ▲
Maternity Allowance †	Industrial benefits	Child Tax Credit	Statutory Adoption Pay ▲
Bereavement Allowance †	War pensions	Working Tax Credit	
Widowed Parent's Allowance ✦ †	Carer's Allowance ✦ †	Housing Benefit	
	Incapacity Benefit (non contributory)/ Severe Disablement Allowance ✢ ✦ †	Council Tax Benefit	
		Health benefits	
		Social Fund	
		Education benefits	

✢ There are both contributory and non-contributory versions of these.

✦ There are Child Dependency Additions to these benefits, but only for people receiving them before 7th April 2003. Claims made after this date will be treated as a claim for Child Tax Credit.

† These benefits are covered by the overlapping benefits rules. These mean that you can only receive the highest of whichever one you qualify for.

▲ You can only receive one of these at one time.

Who is entitled to what benefits

The following list gives some broad indications of the various benefits for different groups of people. People often receive a combination of benefits and may be unclear about which benefits they receive. People must meet the conditions of entitlement for each benefit/tax credit, so this chart does not mean that you qualify for each benefit under the category you fit into.

Older people (aged 60+)	Sickness or disability	Carers
Retirement Pension	Statutory Sick Pay or Incapacity Benefit	Carer's Allowance
Attendance Allowance and/or Disability Living Allowance	Disability Living Allowance	Income Support
State Pension Credit	Income Support	Child Tax Credit
Housing Benefit	Housing Benefit	Housing Benefit
Council Tax Benefit	Council Tax Benefit	Council Tax Benefit
Carer's Allowance	Industrial injury benefits	Health benefits
Bereavement Allowance	War pension or Armed Forces Compensation Scheme	Education benefits
Health benefits	Child Tax Credit	
Education benefits	Working Tax Credit	
Winter Fuel Payment	Health benefits	
	Education benefits	

Unemployed or part-time work (less than 16 hrs pw)	Full-time work (more than 16 hrs pw)	People with children	Bereavement
Jobseeker's Allowance	Working Tax Credit	Child Benefit	Bereavement Allowance/ Widow's Pension
Income Support (if not required to be available for work and to sign on. For example, lone parents)	Child Tax Credit	Child Tax Credit	Widowed Parent's Allowance/ Widowed Mother's Allowance
Child Tax Credit	Housing Benefit	Working Tax Credit	Bereavement Payment
Housing Benefit	Council Tax Benefit	Education benefits	Income Support
Council Tax Benefit	Health benefits	Health benefits	Housing Benefit
Health benefits	Education benefits	All other benefits	Council Tax Benefit
Education benefits			Child Tax Credit
			Working Tax Credit

Making benefit claims

You can make claims for some benefits by using claims forms which are available from social security offices or the DWP website: www.dwp.gov.uk. Tax credits can also be claimed by using the form on HM Revenue and Customs website: www.hmrc.gov.uk. Alternatively, you can start the claim by making a phone call to the relevant organisation.

For certain benefits – Jobseeker's Allowance, Income Support, Incapacity Benefit – you start the claim by phoning your local Jobcentre Plus office. Make sure that your claim is dated from your first call.

When you make a benefit claim you are required to either:

* provide your National Insurance Number or
* provide information to enable your National Insurance Number to be located or
* apply for a National Insurance Number.[1]

There can be delays in obtaining a National Insurance Number and if this holds up your benefit claim, you should ask for an interim payment to be made of the benefit you have claimed.[2] If this is refused, seek independent advice.

If there is a delay in processing your benefits claim, you can ask for an interim payment to be made. For DWP benefits, there is a discretion to make these if your claim has been delayed[3] and if you are a private tenant (including a housing association tenant), the local authority must make an interim payment if they cannot process your claim, unless they have asked you for information or evidence which they reasonably require and you have failed 'without good cause' to supply this information.[4]

Endnotes

1 S 1(1A) & (1B) Social Security Administration Act 1992, & reg 2A Income Support (General) Regulations 1987.

2 Reg 2(1) Social Security (Payments on Account, Overpayments and Recovery) Regulations 1988

3 Reg 2 Social Security (Payments on Account, Overpayments and Recovery) Regulations 1988

4 Reg 93 Housing Benefit Regulations 2006

2 Jobseeker's Allowance

What is Jobseeker's Allowance?

Jobseeker's Allowance (JSA) is a benefit which is paid if you are not working, or working (on average) less than 16 hours a week, and if you are aged between 18 and 65 (for men) or 18 and 60 (for women). Young people aged 16 or 17 face restrictions on when they can receive this – see *Inclusion's* Young Person's Handbook for more details.

You must be:

- capable of working
- available for work
- actively seeking work.

There are two types of JSA:

- Contribution-Based JSA (CJSA) is a non-means-tested benefit. This means that if you have a qualifying National Insurance contribution record you qualify for six months of CJSA. Remember, CJSA is a short-term benefit paid for a maximum of 28 weeks and you can only claim CJSA for yourself (see page 40).
- Income-Based JSA (IBJSA) is a means-tested benefit, so your capital and savings and the circumstances of your partner are taken into account (see page 43). It is calculated in the same way as Income Support.

Who is entitled to Jobseeker's Allowance?

You can receive JSA if you are under 65 (for men) or under 60 (for women) but you cannot usually get JSA if you are aged under 18 (see page 39), you are not working, or work less than 16 hours.

You may also be eligible if:

- You have paid or have been treated as having paid National Insurance contributions: you may be able to get CJSA.
- You are on a low income: you may get IBJSA, even if you have not paid National Insurance contributions. IBJSA is based on how much the law says you need to live on.

You may not be eligible if:

- You are studying full-time (see page 35 for exceptions).
- You receive pay in lieu of notice when a job ends (but you can still make a claim for JSA and receive credits of National Insurance contributions).

Eligibility for Jobseeker's Allowance

There are a number of rules common to both types of JSA. You are eligible for JSA only if you:

- are out of work or working less than 16 hours per week. To qualify for IBJSA, not only must you work less than 16 hours a week, but if you have a partner, they should also work less than 24 hours a week.[1]
- are available for work
- have agreed a Jobseeker's Agreement
- are actively seeking work[2]
- are capable of work (though you can be treated as capable of work if you have been refused Incapacity Benefit on the grounds that you are capable of work and you are appealing against the refusal)
- are not in full-time education
- satisfy the age rules and are resident in the UK.

Are you available for work?[3]

In general you will be accepted as available for work if you can show that you are willing and able to accept at once all offers of employment brought to your notice. Your availability relates to the days and hours you can work as well as the more vague idea of willingness. You will not be expected to look for or accept work as a self-employed person.

You must be available to work for 40 hours a week although this is not set in stone (see below) and your JSA can be suspended immediately if a personal adviser believes that you have failed to demonstrate that you are available for work. Please note if you are on New Deal you will also have to satisfy the available for work condition.

The 40 hour rule

To be available for employment you must be willing and able to take up employment of at least 40 hours per week. You must agree the number of hours you are available with an adviser at your first interview (and these are in your Jobseeker's Agreement) before you will be entitled to receive any JSA. You will need to provide:

- the days of the week you are available to work
- your earliest start time and latest finishing time each day and
- the most hours that you can work each day and in total during the week.[4]

This then becomes known as your pattern of availability.

If you would like to work at least 40 hours per week but are offered work of fewer hours you will be expected to accept it. However, you can refuse any job of less than 24 hours work per week. Similarly, if you have been allowed to restrict your availability to less than 24 hours per week, you will be able to refuse jobs offering less than 16 hours per week.

Restricted availability[5]

You are allowed to be available for less than 40 hours a week in several circumstances if you have:

- caring responsibilities
- a disability or health problem
- been laid off or on short-term work.

You will have to show you are continuing to meet these conditions each time you sign on at the Jobcentre and that you also have a reasonable prospect of obtaining work. You can have additional restrictions if you:

- are within your permitted period
- can show that you have reasonable prospects of securing employment or
- have a sincerely held religious belief or conscientious objection.

The opportunities to place additional restrictions on jobsearch after the permitted period are fairly limited for the majority of customers. You will be able to place restrictions on the nature, rate of pay or location only if you can show that you have reasonable prospects of securing employment notwithstanding your restrictions.

Permitted period[6]

When you become unemployed you may be allowed a short period within which you can restrict your search for work to your usual occupation and to a level of pay that you are used to receiving. This is officially called your permitted period. If you qualify for a permitted period it lasts for a minimum of a week but no longer than 13 weeks from the beginning of your claim. During the permitted period you can also refuse any job offer which is not in your usual occupation or at your accustomed rate of pay. After the permitted period ends, or from the beginning of your claim if you are not granted a permitted period, you must widen the range of jobs you will consider taking and which you can reasonably be expected to do.

The adviser's decision on whether you are allowed a permitted period will be based on the answers you give in the Helping you Back to Work Form (ES2) and the JSA Claim Form (JSA1). The duration of your permitted period will be set out in your Jobseeker's Agreement which is completed by you and an adviser at your interview.

Usual occupation in the permitted period

You will not be given any permitted period if you do not have a usual occupation – such as if you are a school leaver, have never worked before or your former occupation has died out or been replaced. If you have suffered injury or disablement that makes you incapable of resuming your former occupation you will also be ineligible for the permitted period.

However, if you have temporarily left your occupation (e.g. on health grounds or because of a temporary industrial recession) it remains your usual occupation.

If you have received training for an occupation but have not been employed in it you do not qualify for a permitted period. However, if you have undertaken vocational training for at least two months you are allowed a period of four weeks from the end of the training during which you can restrict your jobsearch.

Accustomed rate of pay in the permitted period

When you are within your permitted period you can restrict the rate of pay you are looking for to your accustomed rate of pay (that is the rate of pay in your usual occupation).[7]

Length of permitted period[8]

The length of your permitted period is dependent on several factors, including:

- your usual occupation and any relevant skills or qualifications
- the length of any period of training that you have done which is relevant
- the length of period that you have been employed
- the period since you were last employed and
- the availability and location of employment.

At the end of the permitted period Jobcentre Plus advisers are told that you should be informed at your first interview that if you are still unemployed at the end of this permitted period you will be asked to an advisory interview, at which your Jobseeker's Agreement will be reviewed and revised to take into account the need to broaden your jobsearch.

Restrictions after the permitted period

You can keep restrictions on jobsearch and pay scale after the permitted period if you have shown there are reasonable prospects of securing employment, (please note you can only do this for a maximum period of six months from the beginning of your claim) or if it is reasonable in the light of your physical or mental condition.

The reasonable prospects of employment criteria can also be used to restrict your availability for work. The DWP's benefit Decision Makers are told that any assessment of this should take into account:

Any assessment of this should take into account:

- your skills, qualifications and experience
- the type and number of vacancies within daily travelling distance
- the length of time you have been unemployed
- any job applications you have made and their outcome and
- whether you are willing to move home to take up a job.[9]

The restrictions you place on your availability have a direct relationship to the jobseeking steps that you are expected to undertake (as detailed in your Jobseeker's Agreement).

Restricted availability: some special groups[10]

Certain categories of JSA customer are excused from the requirement that they should be immediately available to take up employment. They are:

- if you have caring responsibilities – defined as caring for someone under 16 or over 65, or care for someone who has mental or physical difficulties – you are permitted to give one week's notice before taking up a job and to be available within 48 hours for a job interview

- if you have a part-time job – if you have a part-time job whilst claiming JSA you are not required to be immediately available for a full-time job provided that you are willing to start a job given 24 hours' notice (or up to a week if you have to give your employer statutory notice). It is possible to continue with your part-time job provided it fits within your pattern of work, which requires the agreement of Jobcentre Plus.

- if you do voluntary work you are permitted to give a week's notice, but you must be available for an interview within 48 hours and

- if you are providing a service – including jury service, being a witness in court proceedings, serving as a justice of the peace or a member of a tribunal, or serving a community service order.

People with caring responsibilities

Under the JSA regulations you must be available for as many hours as your caring responsibilities allow together with the fact that your caring commitments do not get in the way of your having reasonable prospects of securing employment. You must also be available for 16 hours a week or more.

Jobcentre Plus will not accept that someone has caring responsibilities if they are a friend or a neighbour. Caring responsibilities refer to caring for a close relative or those within the same household. If you have children, being available for work means that you should be able to make childcare arrangements within 48 hours and you should have the name of a relative, friend, neighbour or childminder who would be willing to look after your child(ren) or the person(s) you care for within the 24 hour period.

You should carefully consider your options if you have caring responsibilities. People looking after a disabled person who receive Carer's Allowance or lone parents with children aged under 16 may be entitled to claim Income Support (see page 64).

Volunteers

Unemployed people are allowed to do voluntary work. You may even be encouraged to participate in voluntary activity. Voluntary work is defined as work for an organisation whose activities are not-for-profit, and where no payment is received by you except for reasonable expenses, or work for anyone except for a member of your family where no payment is received.

Concessions

In line with the Government's recognition of the importance of voluntary work, there are a number of concessions for volunteers.

Volunteers can give 48 hours' notice before starting a job, or attending a job interview or jobsearch interview. However, you can be contacted at any time by Jobcentre Plus staff. Providers of voluntary work can help you to meet this condition by ensuring that you are contactable all the time that you are a volunteer.

Time spent in voluntary work is also taken into account in deciding on the actively seeking work condition – for example, it may help you develop skills or bring you into contact with people who may be able to offer you a job.

People with disabilities and health problems

Under these exemptions you:

'May restrict...availability in any way providing the restrictions are reasonable in the light of [your] physical or mental condition'[11]

You also do not have to show that you have reasonable prospects of obtaining employment with the restriction so you can restrict the hours you are available for work each week. There is no specified minimum number of weekly hours for which people with disabilities and health problems must be available.

You may also place any other restrictions on the nature, rate of pay, location or other terms and conditions of employment.

While staff can ask for medical evidence to check the validity of your physical or mental condition, they must first check other sources to see if they can gain the necessary information.

Religious beliefs or conscientious objections

You can place restrictions on the type of work (but not the number of hours) that you are available for on the grounds that you have a sincerely-held religious belief or a sincerely-held conscientious objection.[12]

However, unlike JSA customers with disabilities, you must show that you:

'have reasonable prospects of employment notwithstanding these restrictions and meet all the other standard availability rules. Common restrictions in this category are not working on a Sunday on religious grounds or on another day if this is appropriate to your religion. You can also refuse to work in certain jobs (e.g. working in an abattoir or in work which involves the supply and handling of alcohol) because of a conscientious objection or on account of religious beliefs'.

Laid-off and short-time workers

If you are on short-time work or temporarily laid off as a result of adverse industrial conditions encountered by your employer, you are entitled to claim JSA for up to 13 weeks without having to be available for alternative full-time work providing you are willing and able to immediately resume your previous employment.[13] To be counted as laid off or on short time, you must still have a contract of employment with your employer but have had a temporary gap in your work for that employer or a temporary reduction in your hours which the employer will reclaim at a later date.

Casual employment is defined in the benefit rules as work which does not require you to give an employer notice. After 13 weeks the usual rules will apply.

Jobseeker's Agreement

When you first apply for JSA you will be sent or given the forms to complete for your interview and given a date for a new jobseeker interview. At your interview, an adviser will:

- make sure you understand the rules for JSA
- discuss the kinds of work you are looking for
- give you information about jobs, training and other opportunities.

It is at this interview that you agree the Jobseeker's Agreement. Both you and your adviser sign it.

The Jobseeker's Agreement sets out your availability and how you are actively seeking work. The prescribed requirements for a Jobseeker's Agreement include:

- your name
- the hours you are available for employment
- where you are available for employment
- any restrictions on your availability for employment
- a description of the type of employment you are seeking
- the action you will take to seek employment
- the action you will take to improve the prospects of finding employment
- the start and finish dates of any permitted period and
- a statement of rights.

If you are not happy with something in the Jobseeker's Agreement then you should try to re-negotiate it (or take time to seek advice) before you sign it as it is often harder to renegotiate after you have signed it, though you can ask for changes to be made at any stage after signing.[14] You can always ask the supervisor or Decision Maker whether the restrictions you want to place on your agreement are reasonable.

Are you actively seeking work?[15]

You have to take steps each week to find employment.

The details of what you have agreed to do to satisfy the actively seeking work test each week are contained in your Jobseeker's Agreement. The following are regarded as single steps to seek work.

Verbal or written applications for employment to:

- people who have advertised job vacancies
- people who appear to be in a position to offer employment
- employment agencies and employment businesses

or

- Registering with an employment agency or employment business
- Looking for information on job vacancies from advertisements or a person who has advertised a job.

Other single steps:

- appointing a third party to help you look for work
- seeking specialist advice to improve your prospects of finding work (such as from a disability employment adviser)
- drawing up a CV
- drawing up a list of employers to contact about the possibility of a job and/or
- undertaking research about employers.

Please note that the above lists are not exhaustive.

How many steps do you have to take?

You should take more than two steps each week unless one or two steps are all that is reasonable for you to take. (An example might be if you are homeless and are spending most of your time looking for somewhere to live.)

It does not matter whether you take some steps to seek work on every day of the week, or concentrate your activities into a few days (or even one day) providing that you take these steps which are reasonable to satisfy the condition. Circumstances are taken into account to decide whether you are meeting the actively seeking work condition. These include:[16]

- your skills, qualifications and abilities
- your physical or mental condition
- the time which has elapsed since you were last in employment
- your work experience
- the steps you have taken in previous weeks
- the availability and location of vacancies
- whether you are treated as available for employment
- whether you are on or applying to an EU-funded course
- whether you had no living accommodation and
- any time during which you were:
  - carrying out lifeboat or part-time fire-fighting duties
  - engaged in duties for the benefit of others in an emergency
  - attending an Outward Bound course
  - if blind, participating in a course of training in the use of guide dogs
  - if a person with a disability, participating in training in the use of special aids to improve your job prospects
  - engaged in duties with the Territorial Army
  - participating as a part-time student in an employment-related course
  - participating for less than three days in an employment or training programme for which a training allowance is not payable
  - engaged in voluntary work

People who are highly skilled or qualified and who are allowed to restrict their jobsearch (for example because they are within their permitted period) are also given greater flexibility about how they look for work (including registering with specialist employment agencies). Those who are looking for semi-skilled or unskilled work are given less flexibility about how they look for work.

Three tips on meeting the actively seeking work condition

1. At your first interview you will be given a pre-printed jobsearch activity log. You should complete it and show it to the staff who undertake the fortnightly review.

2. Jobseeking evidence can include evidence of direct applications for work, copies of advertisements of jobs about which you have requested details, lists of employers, copies of letters of application or application forms.

3. Jobseeking activities could include drawing up a CV, seeking a reference and obtaining information about potential employers or occupations.

Doubts about your availability to work are more complex. They can be given at any time (including from the way that you answer questions at your first interview). Your Jobseeker's Agreement will only be accepted if the adviser accepts that you meet the availability condition. When you answer questions you must ensure that you meet the availability conditions set out in your Jobseeker's Agreement. This form is the principal monitoring tool. Throughout your claim your availability for work will be examined when you sign on and attend your fortnightly jobsearch review. A more intensive check of this condition is carried out at advisory interviews. Please note that being found to be unavailable for work for just one day of the week is likely to lead to a suspension of benefit.

While your benefit is suspended it is important to continue to demonstrate that you are available for and actively seeking work and attending the Jobcentre Plus office every fortnight to sign on. If your benefit is subsequently reinstated, arrears will be paid only for the days on which you met these conditions.

Actively seeking work and travelling time

For the first thirteen weeks of a JSA claim, you do not have to be available for work which involves more than an hour in each direction. After 13 weeks claiming, you will be expected to take jobs which involve up to one and half hours travel each way and you will also be asked to sign on at the Jobcentre once a week for the next six weeks.

You will receive assistance with fares and overnight costs to attend job interviews if you qualify for the Travel to Interview Scheme (see page 261)

Actively seeking work and special needs

Jobcentre Plus staff are told to be aware of the particular jobsearch difficulties faced by some customers, especially if they have health problems or disabilities, or if they have reading and writing difficulties, or if English is their second language. Specific jobseeking problems should be taken into account by Jobcentre Plus staff.

Actively seeking work and homelessness

Jobcentre Plus staff must take the following factors into account in deciding what jobsearch is reasonable for you to undertake if you are homeless:

- difficulties in contacting employers and employment agencies
- the need to spend time in the week looking for accommodation and
- the fact that you may have less time for active jobsearch and therefore less need to fulfil steps.[17]

Self employment

You are allowed to be available for self-employment provided you are still prepared to take a job as an employee.

The permitted period has been extended to self-employment to reflect this approach. To qualify for restricting your jobsearch in this way, you must have been self-employed at some stage during the last 12 months.

Deliberately avoiding employment

A jobseeking step will not count towards the actively seeking work condition if there is evidence to show that you deliberately reduced your prospects of obtaining employment. Examples given in the guidance are:

- violent or abusive behaviour towards the employer during a job interview
- an inadequate written application for a job

- completion of an inadequate CV
- failure to maintain appropriate behaviour or appearance at a job interview.

However, there is no statutory basis for this, so you should appeal if your benefit is refused on these grounds.

Suspensions

If an adviser believes that such circumstances apply to your jobseeking activity they can suspend your benefit immediately. You will be able to show good cause for your behaviour or appearance in these circumstances only if the decision maker accepts that the circumstances were beyond your control. It may be accepted if you have a history of mental illness. You may also be able to show that inappropriate behaviour on your part was beyond your control as a result of a drink or drug-related condition. However, you will have to substantiate that you have a known problem.

Programmes

New Deal

Under the New Deal you must continue to satisfy the availability for work and the actively seeking work rules whilst undergoing the compulsory initial Gateway scheme. You will continue to get JSA if you do.

After the Gateway, then you will enter one of the New Deal options.

- Employment Option: you will be paid a wage.
- Full-time Education and Training Option: you get an allowance equivalent to your benefit plus £16 a week.
- The Environment and Voluntary Sector Options: you will be paid an allowance or a wage.

If you get a training allowance you retain passported benefits; if you get a wage you will lose JSA although you may be eligible for in-work support such as tax credits (see page 238).

Programmes paying a training allowance

You are treated as available for work and actively seeking work when you attend a programme where you receive a training allowance, such as Work-Based Learning for Adults. You are not required to sign on each fortnight in order to demonstrate that you are available for and actively seeking work (see page 203).

Other government programmes

For other government programmes, you have to remain available for work when you attend them. You are also treated as actively seeking work if you attend any such programme for at least three days per week. For less than three days per week you must still take some steps to satisfy the actively seeking employment condition. It is important to remember that if you are taking a course for less than three days a week, it will affect how your steps towards work are viewed.

Jobsearch reviews

Your jobsearch activity will be checked every fortnight when you have to sign on at Jobcentre Plus and attend a short jobsearch review. At these reviews, Jobcentre Plus staff will call up information you gave at your previous interviews on the computer. The computer prompts the following questions:

... if you say that you have contacted employers about vacancies:

- Which employer?
- How did you contact them?
- Whom did you speak to?
- What happened?

...if you say that you contacted Jobcentre Plus, they are told to ask you:

- Did you call in or ring?
- Whom did you speak to?
- What happened?

Staff will also check what vacancies were available and find out if you followed any of them up, and if not, why not.

Capable of work

To be entitled to JSA you will have to demonstrate that you are capable of work. If you are not capable of work you may be eligible for an incapacity-related benefit such as Incapacity Benefit or Income Support. If you have been judged as capable of work under the Personal Capability Assessment for Incapacity Benefit or Income Support then you must automatically be accepted as being capable of work by Jobcentre Plus without exceptions.[18] This means that you can also appeal against being found fit to work without it affecting your right to JSA.

Short periods of sickness when claiming JSA[19]

You will be able to remain in receipt of JSA for up to two weeks during short periods of illness. You will be required to fill out a form declaring that you are unfit for work.

You will be entitled to JSA in these circumstances on a maximum of two two-week occasions in each 12 month period (based on the date of your initial claim). Once you have been unemployed for more than a year you become eligible again to receive JSA during two periods of sickness in the following 12 months.

Deaths, funerals, domestic emergencies, holidays

You are treated as available for work for the time required to deal with the emergency for a maximum of one week and you are only allowed to make yourself unavailable on these grounds for a maximum of four times in any 12 month period.

For a two week period per year you can take a holiday in the UK which will count as available for work. However, Jobcentre Plus must be able to contact you while you are away from home. In addition, you must be willing to return home immediately to take up a job opportunity.

Signing on[20]

You will have to sign on at the Jobcentre at least once a fortnight (and once a week for six weeks after you have claimed JSA for 13 weeks). Travel expenses to sign on are not payable.

You may sign on by post if you:

- live more than an hour's travel time, door to door, from the nearest Jobcentre
- would have to walk more than three miles to the Jobcentre
- would be absent from home for more than four hours
- have a physical or mental disability which restricts your mobility.

If you don't sign on at the right time or day, your JSA claim stops.[21] If you can show that you had 'good cause' for signing on late within five working days, your claim can continue.[22] However, it is best to sign on at the right time and day to avoid problems.

Education

Full-time study and JSA

You will not be able to claim JSA if you are in full-time education. There are some exceptions:

- If your partner is also a full-time student, you can claim during the long summer vacation providing you or your partner is responsible for a child or young person[23].
- If you are taking a full-time employment related course for no longer than two weeks you can claim JSA providing you have agreed your

attendance with Jobcentre Plus before it started. You will be treated as available for employment and actively seeking employment in any week where you participate for three days or more. Furthermore, you can only take one of these courses in a 12-month period[24].

- If you are following an Open University course and there is a residential element[25].

- You are a full time student who has "abandoned" or been "dismissed" from your course[26] or who has had to stop studying with the agreement of the college/university because of illness or caring responsibilities and is waiting to resume the course after that illness or caring responsibilities have ended[27].

Part-time study and JSA

You may be allowed to undertake part-time study or training while looking for work.

Part-time study is not considered an active step towards finding a job. You are expected to carry out a list of active steps each week to find work in addition to attending your course.

To show that you are available for work, you must be:

- A part-time student
- Willing and able to take time off the course to attend an interview at once and able to be contacted promptly enough for any notification to reach you in time for you to attend the interview
- Willing and able immediately to rearrange the hours of the course to fit in with employment or to give up the course if a job becomes available.

You will normally be expected to agree a pattern of 40 hours a week. In practice the pattern of availability you agree with the Jobcentre Plus adviser will depend on the type of work you are looking for. For example, if you have been allowed to restrict yourself to shop work your adviser may insist that your pattern of availability includes Saturdays. It is important that your part-time study fits with your pattern of availability.

Your availability for work should not be affected if the hours of your course or training fall completely outside your agreed pattern of availability. It is your responsibility to inform your local Jobcentre Plus if you have enrolled or intend to enrol on a course. When you first sign on for JSA you are asked this question in the Helping you Back to Work form. Afterwards you could be asked about part-time study when your jobsearch activities are reviewed at Restart and other interviews.

When you tell the Jobcentre Plus adviser that you are taking or that you intend to take a course, you will be given a questionnaire to complete. This form will test whether you can follow your part-time course and continue to receive benefit by applying up to three separate tests to your claim:

1. Are you a part-time student?

2. Are you available for and actively seeking employment under Regulation 11?

3. If Regulation 11 does not apply (see below), can you be treated as available for and actively seeking employment when matters relating to the course are taken into account?

1. If you are judged to be a full-time student you will not be entitled to JSA. The definition of full-time student differs depending on where in the UK you attend the course, the level of the course and who funds it. Some young people aged under 20 who are in full time non-advanced education may be able to receive Income Support – for example, they have to live away from parents and are estranged or they are a lone parent or they have a disability. If you are not sure how your course is funded, you should ask the welfare officer where you attend your course. Most courses are funded or part-funded, in England, by the Learning and Skills Council or the equivalent in Scotland, Wales or Northern Ireland. Their rules are that full-time study involves more than 16 guided learning hours per week (a slightly different definitions apply in Scotland and Northern Ireland). This will be shown on your learning agreement (every student has one). This contains the number of weekly guided learning hours, the name of the college/course provider, your personal details and the signature college/course provider. Jobcentre Plus staff

will accept a copy of the learning agreement from you. Time spent on unpaid work experience which is part of your course does not normally fall within the definition of guided learning hours. For higher education courses there is no hourly definition of full-time.

2. The second test – Regulation 11[28] – makes it easier for some part-time students or trainees to keep benefit. It allows the fact that the hours of your course are wholly, or partly, within the times you have agreed you will be available for work to be ignored. You qualify for Regulation 11 if you have been allowed to restrict your hours of availability by Jobcentre Plus because of:

- Your physical or mental health, or
- Your caring responsibilities, or
- You are working short time, or
- Your restrictions still leave you available for work for at least 40 hours a week.

In addition you must meet one of the following tests:

- For a period of three months immediately before the course you were receiving JSA (or income support or Incapacity Benefit because you were incapable of work).
- In the six months before starting your course you met one of those conditions for a total of three months and in between you were working full time or earning too much to receive benefit.

If you satisfy Regulation 11 you will not have to move onto the third test.

3. If you do not qualify for Regulation 11, Jobcentre Plus will apply the third and stricter test to your claim. Under this third test, Jobcentre Plus staff will ask questions about your course and take your answers into account in deciding whether you are available for work. For example, if you can rearrange the hours of your course by doing evening classes or open learning, to fit around a job, you are more likely to qualify.

Certain expense payments associated with taking a course can be disregarded as income for the purposes of JSA and Income Support.

Age and residency rules

In order to claim JSA you must be under pensionable age. Once you reach pensionable age you should claim retirement pension (or Pension Credit when you reach the age of 60).

16 and 17 year olds

16 and 17 year olds will find that their eligibility is restricted as they are unlikely to satisfy the National Insurance contribution requirements for CJSA and there are special rules for people under 18 who claim IBJSA. Further information can be found in *Inclusion's* Young Person's Handbook. However, it is still possible for many 16 and 17 year olds to make successful claims.

Presence in the UK

Generally you must be present in the UK to be eligible for JSA although you may be able to claim CJSA whilst in the EU if you have been claiming CJSA and have been signing on as available for work for at least four weeks before you go abroad, are going abroad to look for work, and register within seven days as unemployed with the employment service of the other country. Please note that you may have to get advice before going abroad from your local Jobcentre Plus office. You may also go abroad and keep JSA for a job interview, and to take a child or young person for whom you receive benefits or tax credits abroad for medical treatment for up to eight weeks, for NHS treatment. You must inform Jobcentre Plus if you think any of these might apply to you.[29]

People from abroad

If you are from abroad, have worked in the UK and paid National Insurance contributions then you can claim CJSA like anyone else.

If you are from an EU country you may want to claim your unemployment benefit from that country and have it paid via the Jobcentre Plus Office.

You may also use National Insurance contributions paid in another EU country, or a country which has a Reciprocal Agreement with the UK and which covers JSA or to aggregate contributions paid in that country with any paid in the UK to qualify for CJSA in the UK.

To qualify for IBJSA you will need to have a right to reside in the UK (for example, because you have worked in the UK) and to be habitually resident.

For further information, see *Inclusion's* Newcomer's Handbook.

Types of JSA

There are two types of JSA:

1. Contribution-based JSA (CJSA)

2. Income-based JSA (IBJSA)

CJSA

- CJSA is non-means-tested so your earnings and savings and the circumstances of your partner are irrelevant.
- You receive CJSA if you have paid enough of the right National Insurance contributions.
- CJSA is a short-term benefit paid at a fixed rate based on your age for a maximum of six months.
- You can only claim CJSA for yourself.
- The amount of CJSA you get may be reduced if you have an occupational or personal pension above £50 a week.
- If you are entitled to CJSA, but your income is still below the minimum level of income the law says you need to live on, you may be able to get some IBJSA.

National Insurance contribution conditions

There are two National Insurance contribution conditions that you must meet to qualify for CJSA:

1. You must have paid Class 1 contributions for one of the last two complete tax years before the beginning of the benefit year in which your JSA claim began and these earnings must total at least 25 times the Lower Earnings Limit during that tax year and

2. You must have paid Class 1 contributions and/or been credited with Class 1 contributions for both of the previous two tax years before the beginning of the benefit year in which your JSA claim began and these earnings and/or credits must total at least 50 times the Lower Earnings Limit during each tax year.

The jargon explained

The Lower Earnings Limit is the level of weekly earnings on which you begin to pay National Insurance contributions as an employee. It changes every year. For 2007–8 the Lower Earnings Limit is £87 per week. If you earn between £87.01 and £100 a week, you will not pay National Insurance contributions but will be treated as having paid them (which means you may use them to receive benefits).

Class 1 contributions are paid by employees. Self-employed people, who pay Class 2 and Class 4 contributions, cannot qualify for CJSA (though they may still qualify for CJSA using Class 1 Contributions paid when they were an employee in previous years).

Contribution credits are automatically paid when you are signing on as unemployed. Each weekly credit that you receive represents a Class 1 contribution on earnings equivalent to the Lower Earnings Limit in that year. You can meet the second contribution condition even if you were not earning (or only earning for part of the tax year) if you have enough contribution credits.

The benefit year is based on the calendar year but begins on the first Sunday in January and ends on the Saturday immediately before the first Sunday in the following calendar year.

The tax year begins on 6 April and runs through to 5 April of the following year.

Duration of CJSA

CJSA lasts for a maximum of 28 weeks. If you are unemployed for longer than this you will continue to receive benefit only if you qualify for IBJSA.

Breaks in claim

If you are claiming CJSA and you sign off for less than 12 weeks, the JSA linking rule states that you have not broken your claim. Your entitlement will resume on the same basis from where you left off.

If you are claiming CJSA and break your claim for more than 12 weeks you are then treated as a fresh claim and have to requalify.

Part, or (in some cases), all of your six month entitlement to CJSA can be used up during any period when CJSA is not payable because of a sanction. In principle, this means that you can lose all your entitlement to CJSA if you are sanctioned at the beginning of a claim for leaving a job voluntarily or because of misconduct and a Decision Maker imposes the maximum six month sanction.

You can also be treated as being in receipt of CJSA if you meet the contribution conditions but do not receive any payment due to the income you are getting from an occupational or personal pension. Your CJSA is cut pound for pound for any weekly pension above £50 a week.

Re-qualifying for CJSA

To requalify for a new period of entitlement to CJSA:

- Your last claim for CJSA must have ended more than 12 weeks previously.
- The National Insurance contribution test must be applied to at least one new tax year which was not used in your most recent claim for CJSA.
- You must meet all the National Insurance contribution conditions again using the new tax year(s).

Because a new tax year must be used for your contribution test if you are to re-qualify for CJSA this means that you will not be able to make a new claim in the same benefit year. As a result, in some cases it may be worth delaying reapplying for CJSA if you know that you will requalify shortly by claiming in a new benefit year.

IBJSA

IBJSA is means-tested and you can claim for your partner and children.

You receive IBJSA regardless of previous National Insurance contributions.

It is possible to register and sign on regularly as unemployed and look for work without receiving JSA and you might want to do this so that your National Insurance record is credited. However, most people claim one type of JSA.

IBJSA rules

IBJSA is a means-tested benefit so your capital and your partner's circumstances are taken into account.

How is IBJSA calculated?

The means test for IBJSA is identical to that for Income Support. See page 67.

Also see the benefit rates table (page 276) for further information.

The means test

According to the rules of the means test you will not qualify for any IBJSA in any week where:

- your partner works for 24 hours or more a week
- the total capital (e.g. savings and lump sum redundancy payments) held by you and/or your partner is in excess of £16,000
- your and/or your partner's income in any week is more than your total weekly payment from IBJSA.

Weekly income from other sources as well as part-time work is taken into account for IBJSA. Once your weekly income has been calculated, your IBJSA will be cut by the amount of net earnings minus an 'earnings disregard' of between £5 and £20 depending on your circumstances plus half of any pension payments you are making.

If you or your family has capital above £16,000 you will not qualify for any IBJSA. If you or your family has capital between £6,000 and £16,000, then £1 is deducted from your IBJSA for every £250 of capital above the £6,000 mark. For example, capital of £7,500 would lead to a weekly cut of £6 in your IBJSA.

Even if you only receive a small amount of IBJSA, you are automatically eligible for:

- free prescriptions,
- free school meals,
- free dental care,
- free sight tests and glasses,
- milk and vitamin tokens if you have children under school age or
- for expectant and nursing mothers,
  - refunds of fares for hospital visits,
  - Social Fund grants and loans and
  - maximum Housing Benefit.

National Insurance credits

When you are out of work and are not paying National Insurance contributions, gaps appear in your National Insurance record. These can affect your future entitlement to benefits. In many circumstances you are automatically given credits to cover periods when you are not working, for example, if you have been a student or cared for someone with severe disabilities.

You also receive these credits automatically when you are unemployed and signing on for JSA. However, if your entitlement to JSA is completely disallowed because of any income, earnings, or savings, you are no longer entitled to your contribution credits unless you continue to sign on for them. This may affect you if you do not qualify for any JSA because you fail to qualify for IBJSA under the means test and you are not receiving CJSA. In these circumstances you are normally advised to continue signing on even though you are not entitled to any money in order to be awarded weekly National Insurance contribution credits.

You may not be directly encouraged by Jobcentre Plus staff to sign on for your credits. However, it is your right to do so and it can be important for your future entitlement to contributory benefits (especially Retirement Pension).

How to claim JSA

You should claim JSA at your local Jobcentre Plus office. The first contact is normally by phone and you will have a short initial interview by phone and be sent or given the forms to complete for your interview and given a date for a new jobseeker interview at the Jobcentre Plus office. If you need help filling in any Jobcentre Plus forms the Jobcentre Plus should do this for you and also arrange for you to have an interpreter if you need one.[30] You should try to bring along relevant evidence and information – for example, letters about your employment ending, your P45, and evidence about income and savings if you are claiming IBJSA. Do not delay your claim if you do not have all the information to hand as this can be sent later.

If you received JSA within the last 12 weeks, you can use a shorter claim form. This is known as 'Rapid Reclaim'.

At your interview an adviser will:

- make sure you understand the rules for JSA
- discuss the kinds of work you are looking for
- give you information about benefits, jobs, training and other opportunities.

It is at this interview that you agree to the Jobseeker's Agreement. Both you and your adviser sign it.

JSA is different from most other benefits because you have to demonstrate that you meet the conditions of entitlement in order to get it. You do this by signing on every two weeks, which also involves a short jobsearch review (now officially called your fortnightly review). At longer intervals, you must also go to more detailed interviews.

Once you have been unemployed for about 13 weeks you will be called in for your first in-depth advisory interview at which you will be asked questions about your jobseeking. After this, the main advisory interview you will have to attend is the Restart interview, which is compulsory for everyone and takes place every six months. At each six-monthly interview you become eligible for employment programmes which are detailed throughout this book.

If Jobcentre Plus staff think that you require more assistance with your jobseeking, or if they think that you may be working while claiming and not declaring all your earnings, you may be required to attend additional compulsory advisory interviews. This may happen because a member of staff is not satisfied or because you may be caseloaded. This means a Jobcentre Plus adviser gives you more attention.

Joint claims

If you are a member of a couple (including a same sex couple who live together as a couple), have no children and were born after 28 October 1957 you will both have to jointly claim IBJSA and both will have to meet the conditions of entitlement.[31] (Note: the joint claim rules only apply to IBJSA, not CJSA). If one of you fails to meet the conditions for entitlement then there are special rules for reducing benefit and paying it to the customer who does meet them. If one of you is sanctioned (see page 61) your IBJSA will be reduced by half.

If you are a joint claim couple, and one of you fits into a certain category, then that person will not have to meet the labour market rules for JSA. The most common categories are:[32]

- working 16-24 hours per week
- some carers
- aged 60 or older

- incapable for work because of illness or disability
- mentally or physically disabled with earnings or hours of work reduced to 75% or less of people who don't have a disability
- registered blind
- incapable of work because of pregnancy

Three common problems with JSA claims

1. Payments at the end of a job

2. Trade disputes

3. Income Tax

1 If you receive holiday pay or pay-in-lieu of notice/wages you will be treated as if you are still in work and not normally entitled to JSA (though you may qualify for National Insurance Credits). However, do not delay making a claim as it is not only possible to claim JSA up to three months in advance,[33] (thus dealing with the bureaucracy of making a new claim and to be paid JSA when you are entitled with less delay) but you may also qualify for National Insurance Credits during your pay-in-lieu period. Redundancy pay, to which you have a contractual right, can also affect your JSA, but other redundancy payments will normally be treated as capital.[34] Seek advice if you are unsure.

2. If you withdraw your labour, or have a direct interest in a trade dispute at your place of work for any day, you are not entitled to claim JSA for the week which includes that day. You can become entitled to JSA during the dispute if you get another bona fide job and then lose that second job. Your dependants may also have entitlements. You should get advice from your trade union.

3. You may be entitled to a refund of some or all of the Income Tax you have paid after the end of the tax year in which you claimed JSA or if you return to work within the same tax year. Jobcentre Plus should issue you with form P45U which you should send to your Tax Office after the end of the tax year or give to your new employer.

Leaving a job

Leaving a job voluntarily

The benefit rules state that you will be sanctioned from JSA and lose your benefit for between one and 26 weeks if a benefit Decision Maker decides that you have voluntarily left your job without just cause.[35] The sanctions cannot apply if you have left self-employment.

Voluntary departure or dismissed for misconduct?

You should immediately sign on for JSA even if you think you will encounter problems, as you may win on appeal and you may also qualify for IBJSA on hardship grounds and/or other benefits – for example, Housing Benefit.

The voluntary unemployment sanction applies to previous jobs within the last six months and also applies to you if you refuse to apply for or accept employment.

There are a number of factors taken into account when working out the length of a sanction and there may also be an overlap of sanctions.

Causes for leaving a job voluntarily

You must show just cause to avoid a benefit sanction.

You must normally show that you went through the various processes and procedures to try and correct the situation before deciding to leave a job.

- You can have just cause if your employer tries to impose a change in the terms and conditions of employment 'without agreement and which makes them less favourable than before, they may have ended the employment by breaking the contract of employment'. Pay cannot be a reason and there are other caveats.
- You can show just cause for leaving a job if you 'had a genuine and substantial grievance about the employment and had tried in a proper and reasonable way to get it settled'. For example, you may have been asked to do work which is not covered by your contract of

employment.

- You will have just cause if your 'employer ordered you to do something that conflicted with your sincerely held religious or conscientious principles'.
- Personal and domestic circumstances can be used as just cause provided they are pressing, for example, if you had to look after your child, although this may conflict with other elements of your Jobseeker's Agreement
- You can show just cause if you give up for health reasons. This could be through the job being either beyond your physical or mental capacity or harmful to your health. Medical confirmation is preferred but not required.
- Moving home beyond the daily travelling distance of your job does not give you just cause for voluntary leaving unless 'there was some urgent personal reason' for the move, for example, illness.
- Leaving for another job could be just cause if you had a firm offer of another job which started immediately and the new job falls through unexpectedly or doesn't last long. There are again several caveats that need to be considered.
- Giving up a new line of work which you are unsuited to will be just cause, particularly if it is done during the early weeks of a job because it prevents an employer from having an unsuitable employee.
- Taking voluntary redundancy where there is a need for redundancies by your employer should not be viewed as leaving voluntarily.

Employment lost through misconduct

There is no definition of misconduct, but some examples include wilful disobedience of instructions, failure to observe rules and regulations, refusal to perform particular work, negligence, carelessness or inefficient work, offensive behaviour, dishonesty, unauthorised absence or bad time keeping, disqualification from driving (if employed in a driving capacity) and the conviction of a criminal offence inside or outside work.

If you have been dismissed without a warning, for being a 'slow worker' or in unfair circumstances, you may be able to argue that a sanction should not be imposed because you did not lose your job through 'misconduct'.

The procedure

Jobcentre Plus will send an ES85 form to your employer. They do not have to complete this, but if they do it will give information about why you left your job.

You must be allowed to comment on your employer's allegations by writing a response in the ES86LV form and it is important that you do provide comments. This form must be returned to the Jobcentre Plus office within seven days of the date of issue if your comments are to be taken into account by the benefits Decision Maker.

This process can be bypassed by issuing you directly with an ES84 form, which also requests details of how you left your last job. If you are taking action against your employer for discrimination or unfair dismissal, you should seek legal advice before replying to enquiries from Jobcentre Plus. If your employer gives Jobcentre Plus different reasons for dismissal from those given to you, this may be significant for your unfair dismissal claim. A JSA sanction operates independently of an unfair dismissal hearing/decision by an Employment Tribunal.

Once all the evidence is submitted Jobcentre Plus will send you a Notification of Adjudication Submission letter (ES48S). If you are to be sanctioned, this letter should also contain a copy of the leaflet JSA9 that explains how to apply for hardship payments. If you receive one of these letters you should immediately tell a Jobcentre Plus member of staff that you want to apply for a hardship payment and you should also appeal both against the sanction and the length of the sanction (it is possible to have the length of the sanction reduced or to have the whole sanction removed). These appeals have a high success rate.

Employment on Trial

Employment on Trial is a concessionary period during which you can leave a job voluntarily and be sure that you will not be disqualified under the voluntary unemployment sanction.[36]

To qualify you must have been unemployed for at least 13 weeks before you started the job, leave the job from the beginning of the fifth week onwards but no later than the end of the 12th week and have been working for 16 hours a week or more.[37] Vocational training such as WBLA also counts toward the qualifying period of 13 weeks.

Suspension of JSA and other sanctions

If it is felt that you are not actively seeking or being available for work, Jobcentre Plus advisers are instructed to immediately suspend your benefit[38] and to give you a Notification of an Entitlement Doubt letter (Jobcentre Plus 48). This letter says how long JSA will be suspended for (one week minimum) and whether you can apply for hardship payments of IBJSA.

You will only get money from the beginning of the suspension period (or the beginning of your claim) if you qualify for hardship payments as someone from a vulnerable group or if it is accepted that you were available for and/or actively seeking work.

If you are not classified as being in a vulnerable group, you can apply for hardship payments of IBJSA only after your JSA has been suspended for two weeks. In some cases this means that you will not be able to apply for hardship payments during the whole period of suspension (e.g. if you lose JSA for one or two weeks for not actively seeking work).

Whatever the circumstances, if you are not receiving any money, you should immediately ask to make an application for an IBJSA hardship payment. If you are told that you cannot do so because your claim has been terminated, you should then ask to make a new claim for JSA.

If your JSA is suspended for not actively seeking work, it is normally only suspended for one or two weeks. Jobcentre Plus staff are told to explain that your jobsearch activity will be reviewed again when you next attend the Jobcentre Plus office so it is in your interests to demonstrate that you meet the actively seeking work/availability condition.

It is very important to appeal against any sanctions or benefit suspensions. If you can find someone to represent you at the appeal hearing, you have a good chance of success.

Refusing employment

You can be disqualified from JSA for up to six months (and for a minimum of one week) if the Jobcentre Plus Office can show that without 'good cause', you refuse or fail to apply for a job vacancy which Jobcentre Plus has informed you about. You can also be sanctioned if you are offered the job in such a vacancy but you refuse to take it without good cause.

You cannot be sanctioned if you refuse a job lasting less than 24 hours per week (or a job of less than 16 hours per week if you have been allowed to restrict your availability for work in your Jobseeker's Agreement to less than 24 hours a week).

The meaning of refusing employment for the purposes of imposing a benefit sanction is much wider than simply refusing or failing to apply for or accept a job notified to you by Jobcentre Plus. It includes behaving in such a way that you lose the chance of employment. This might be if you do not turn up or arrive late at an interview, go to the wrong place through your own negligence, impose unreasonable conditions on acceptance of a job, behave or appear at the interview in such a way that the employer decides not to offer you the job, refuse to give references, delay acceptance of the job until it has been taken by someone else or accept a job but then fail to start on the agreed day.

Moreover, Jobcentre Plus staff now have the power under the Jobseeker's Direction to instruct you to improve your employability by taking steps to present yourself acceptably to employers.

The vacancy must be notified to you personally by a Jobcentre Plus member of staff. You cannot show good cause for refusing a vacancy on the grounds that you were not given enough details about it when you were notified.

If you are offered work by employment agencies or external providers, for example, programme centres or Connexions/Careers Offices run by outside companies, vacancies are not classed as notified to you by the Jobcentre Plus. However, if Jobcentre Plus staff become aware that you have been offered a vacancy by an external agency, they are within their rights to offer it to you again. This changes it to a vacancy that has been officially notified to you by Jobcentre Plus. The same applies for other types of vacancies, such as jobs from a newspaper.

Reading a job advertisement on the self-service boards in a Jobcentre Plus office does not constitute notification of a vacancy. They need to be discussed personally with you by a member of Jobcentre Plus staff.

You cannot be sanctioned for refusing employment which is vacant because of a stoppage of work due to a trade dispute.

You cannot be disqualified under the refusal of employment rule for refusing or failing to follow up self-employed jobs. However, if you are restricting your jobsearch during your permitted period to self-employment, neglecting to follow up these types of vacancy may call into question whether you are available for and actively seeking work.

You can be sanctioned if you refuse or fail to accept a temporary job notified by Jobcentre Plus.

You can be sanctioned for up to six months for refusing to take up an employed-status place on Work-Based Learning for Adults (WBLA). However, this does not apply if you are participating on WBLA as a non-employed trainee (that is, you are on a training allowance consisting of your benefit plus £10).

Refusing a reasonable opportunity of work

The same benefit sanction for refusing employment can also be imposed for neglecting to avail yourself without 'good cause' of a reasonable opportunity of employment in your previous employment.[39]

'Neglect to avail yourself' of employment means that you have refused to take advantage of a reasonable opportunity of work that has arisen with a previous employer.

Some of the issues in deciding whether you have good cause to refuse employment or neglect to avail yourself of an opportunity are:[40]

- The job offer is less than 24 hours per week or 16 hours for some customers. (Jobs with 24 hours in one week and less in others are considered less than 24 hour a week jobs.)

- You have recently undergone training for a particular kind of employment for a period of not less than two months (you can refuse work for up to four weeks from the day your training ends).
- The vacancy does not conform to any of your restrictions on your availability for work (set out in your Jobseeker's Agreement).
- The vacancy does not conform to the restrictions that you have placed on the type of employment and level of pay during your permitted period.
- The vacancy would cause you health problems or excessive physical or mental stress (the best evidence would come from your doctor or an allied professional).
- You have a sincerely held religious or conscientious objection (you must give evidence both that it genuinely conflicts with your principles and that it is a sincere objection).
- You have caring responsibilities that would make the job unreasonable. (Inconvenience is not enough for good cause – it must be an unreasonable stipulation. Examples include working at night, having a very early start or finish or if the job requires overnight stays away from home. Good cause would also be given if it conflicts with your restrictions on availability or the 48 hours' notice you can give before taking up employment. In addition, you cannot be sanctioned if you refuse a vacancy lasting less than 16 hours per week if you have restricted your availability to less than 24 hours per week.)
- The travelling time is excessive (for example, over one and half hours after the 13 weeks claiming JSA).
- The work-based expenses incurred would represent an unreasonably high proportion of the wages of the job.
- Some customers from specific groups can refuse employment if it conflicts with their availability or notice period (see above).
- The rate of pay is not a reason for good cause but must, of course, be in line with the National Minimum Wage legislation. Examples of reasons linked to income and outgoings which would not give you good cause are particularly high financial commitments, the fact that you

or a member of your household would lose the right to other benefits and concessions which are available to unemployed people. There are exemptions. These include when you are within your permitted period, when you have been allowed to restrict your rate of pay for the first six months, when you have been allowed to restrict your level of pay on health grounds, if the job pays on a commission-only basis and if the work-based expenses would be unreasonably high.

- The previous points cover good causes in the benefit regulations. Any matter you put forward must however be considered. This includes if you have a definite chance of another job that will start in the near future, is likely to last as long and will be lost if you accept the job offer.

This is not an exhaustive list.

Jobseeker's Direction

The Jobseeker's Direction (which must be reasonable in regard to your circumstances) is a power which enables Jobcentre Plus staff to require you, under threat of a sanction, to take particular action aimed at improving your chances of finding employment.[41]

It must be given in writing in order to qualify as a Direction.

If you refuse or fail to comply with a Direction which is reasonable, and cannot show good cause, your JSA personal allowance is cut for two weeks. This is the same sanction that is imposed if you do not attend a compulsory programme (see page 58).

Though the law does not list them, Jobseeker's Directions fall into one of the following four categories:

- your jobsearch activities
- referral to Jobcentre Plus programmes
- referral to other employment and training programmes
- your behaviour and appearance (it may be possible to challenge this using Human Rights law).

Jobsearch activities can include applying for a specific vacancy (typically part-time), applying for advertised vacancies not notified to Jobcentre Plus, sending your CV to a particular employer and making speculative approaches to employers in a particular trade.

A Jobseeker's Direction can be used to refer you to employment and training programmes which you may not wish to attend and which under normal circumstances are not compulsory. However, it is emphasised to advisers that Directions should not be used indiscriminately to refer customers to Jobcentre Plus programmes.

If you are instructed to apply for a job under 24 hours a week you must do that otherwise you can be sanctioned for a two or four week period for not complying with a Jobseeker's Direction. However, you cannot be sanctioned for refusing an offer of employment after you apply for a job which is for less than 24 hours per week. So you should follow the Jobseeker Direction, but you can refuse the job offer.

Directions involving behaviour and appearance can be given, where you have between two and four weeks to comply. This will only occur if advice from Jobcentre Plus staff is ignored. No personal directions that are discriminatory because of gender, sexuality, religion, disability, race or nationality or would be at odds with conscientious belief can be given. An example of this type of direction would be if you have a nose ring and the adviser knows that a certain employer will not tolerate nose rings, then you would be told to either remove the nose ring or to change your job goals.

How and when can a Jobseeker's Direction be issued?

Jobcentre Plus advisers can give a Jobseeker's Direction at any stage of the claim. However, they should not issue one when a referral to a Decision Maker is more appropriate, as a means of filling programmes, when it is unlawfully discriminatory, when at odds with a sincerely held conscientious belief.

Good cause for not carrying out a Direction

A benefit sanction can only be imposed on you for refusing or failing to carry out a Direction if:

- the Direction was given in writing to you by a Jobcentre Plus adviser
- the Direction was reasonable taking your circumstances into account
- you were not referred to a vacancy resulting from a stoppage due to a trade dispute and
- you do not have good cause for refusal or failure.

All the guidance on good cause for refusing employment is equally applicable to employment-related Jobseeker's Directions with one exception – you do not have good cause for refusing or failing to carry out a Direction because the employment in question is less than 24 hours (or less than 16 hours in certain circumstances (see page 52)).

In addition, certain restrictions on the employment you are available for (for example if you are within the permitted period) may simultaneously give you good cause for refusing or failing to carry out Directions.

You can refuse to undertake a training-related Direction (for four weeks from your end date) if you have recently undergone training for a period of not less than two months and the Direction is intended to find you a different type of employment.

Good cause justifications

You will have good cause for refusing to comply with a Direction for the following reasons:

- health reasons
- conflict with a sincerely held religious or conscientious objection
- conflict with caring responsibilities
- if the expenses in carrying out the Jobseeker's Direction were unreasonably high.

Good cause considerations include:

- any availability restrictions imposed by you which have been accepted
- any medical conditions or personal circumstances which have been accepted or

- any religious or conscientious belief such as
  - religious objections to handling alcohol or certain foodstuffs,
  - religious objections to working on a certain day,
  - objections to working with materials which may be used for the destruction of life or
  - religious objections to working with the opposite sex.

Compulsory programmes

Do you have to participate in employment and training schemes?

During your fortnightly review, and especially at advisory interviews, you are likely to be offered information about government-funded training and employment schemes such as the New Deal for Young People.

Most of the New Deal programmes for the unemployed are compulsory and you will be subject to benefit sanctions if you have been notified by Jobcentre Plus staff about a vacancy and you refuse to participate or fail to attend without 'good cause'.[42]

Jobcentre Plus advisers also have powers to issue a Jobseeker's Direction to refer you to a programme.

You can be sanctioned if you refuse, without good cause, to attend a compulsory scheme, if you leave early, if you are dismissed for misconduct or if your behaviour means you lose the chance of a place. This includes turning up late at an interview with a provider, going to the wrong place through your own negligence, imposing unreasonable conditions on acceptance of a place on a programme, behaving in such a manner at the interview that the provider decides not to offer you a place, delaying acceptance of a place on a programme until it has been taken by someone else or accepting a place on a programme but then failing to start on the agreed day.

You will be judged to have left a programme early if you have an unauthorised absence of just one day.

Compulsory programmes: sanctions

If you have been referred to a compulsory programme or to a voluntary scheme under a Jobseeker's Direction, your JSA can be cut for two or four weeks. The cut to your benefit is automatically for four weeks if you have already had a sanction in the previous 12 months. Otherwise, it is for two weeks. Your benefit cannot be cut until a decision maker has examined all the evidence and written to you to get your version of events and comment on any evidence which is being used against you. It is important that you comment on any evidence.

What happens if you change your mind?

If you originally refused or failed to take up a place on a compulsory programme and subsequently changed your mind and took up the place before the provider had filled it and before the course had started, you can be exempted from a benefit sanction or have it revised in your favour.

Good cause for not attending a compulsory programme[43]

This includes:

- if you have a physical or mental health problem which meant that you could not attend or your attendance would put at risk the health of others on the scheme or would have put your health or safety at risk
- if you have a sincerely-held religious or conscientious objection
- if the travelling time to the scheme is over an hour each way, is a long distance from home or if it would be very difficult for you to attend
- if you have caring responsibilities and no close relative available to care
- if you are attending court for jury service or appearing as a witness
- if you are attending the funeral of a close relative or close friend or dealing with an emergency.

Losing a place on a Compulsory Programme because of misconduct

The same law about the meaning of misconduct and loss of employment applies to you whether or not you will be sanctioned if you lose your place on a Compulsory Programme because of alleged misconduct. See page 49.

The procedure

The penalty process for refusal of employment, neglect to avail, refusing a Jobseeker's Direction or failing to attend a compulsory programme is as follows:

- If Jobcentre Plus staff decide to submit you for a benefit sanction they are legally obliged to give you the opportunity to comment on the circumstances on an official form. This is sent to the Decision Maker and must be used in deciding if you had good cause for your actions. If you demonstrate this is the case, you should not have a sanction imposed.

- If a sanction is imposed, the evidence you provide may reduce the length of the sanction period. The form that you receive will give you the opportunity to give your reasons and to provide good cause but you will have to complete it and return it to the Jobcentre Plus Office within seven days of it being issued (not received). It is important that you give your views.

- You should continue to sign on. Your JSA will be cut only if the decision maker finds against you and is obliged to inform you by sending you a notice. You should also apply for a hardship payment.

- You may also wish to request a revision of the decision or appeal against the decision. Many appeals are successful, especially if you attend or have someone to help you and you may also appeal against the length of a sanction as well as the sanction itself.

Ways to deal with sanctions

- Always seek independent advice and appeal against a sanction – most appeals succeed.
- Continue to sign on as unemployed.
- Reply quickly to enquiries from Jobcentre Plus, if necessary, seek independent advice before replying.
- Do not delay making a claim if you think you may be sanctioned.
- If you have been sanctioned and you have a partner and you are also not a Joint Claim Couple (see page 46), it may be possible to avoid a sanction if they qualify for JSA and they make claim instead of you.

- Do you qualify for another benefit instead of JSA? Sanctions only apply to JSA and you will not be sanctioned, for example, if you qualify for Income Support rather than IBJSA.

Endnotes

1   Reg 51 Jobseeker's Allowance Regulations 1996 (JSA Regs)

2   Ss 6, 7 8 & 9 Jobseeker's Act 1995 (JS Act) & regs 18, 23 & 31 JSA Regs.

3   Regs 5-16 JSA Regs

4   Reg 31 JSA Regs

5   Regs 7 – 10 JSA Regs

6   Reg 16 JSA Regs

7   Reg 16(1) JSA Regs

8   Reg 16(2) JSA Regs

9   Reg 10(1) JSA Regs

10 Reg 5 JSA Regs

11 Reg 13(3) JSA Regs

12 Reg 13(2) JSA Regs

13 Reg 17 JSA Regs

14 S10 JS Act

15 Reg 18 JSA Regs

16 Reg 19(3) JSA Regs

17 Reg 18(3) (j) JSA Regs

18 Reg 10 Social Security and Child Support (Decisions and Appeals) Regulations 1999 and schedule 1 para 2 JS Act

19 Reg 55 JSA Regs

20 Regs 23 & 24 JSA Regs

21 Regs 25 & 26 JSA Regs

22 Reg 27 JSA Regs

23 Reg 15 JSA Regs

24 Reg 14 JSA Regs

25 Reg 14 JSA Regs

26 Reg 1 (3A) (b) JSA Regs

27 Reg 1(3D) JSA Regs

28 Reg 11 JSA Regs

29 Reg 14 JSA Regs

[30] Page 10 of leaflet published by DWP: 'Jobcentre Plus. Our Service Standards.'

[31] Reg 3A JSA Regs

[32] Schedule A1 JSA Regs

[33] Reg 13(1) Social Security (Claims and Payments) Regulations 1987

[34] Reg 52(3) JSA Regs

[35] S19 (6) (a) & (b) JS Act

[36] S20(3) JS Act

[37] Reg 74(4) JSA Regs

[38] Reg 16 (2) Social Security and Child Support (Decisions and Appeals) Regulations 1999

[39] S 19(6) (d) JS Act

[40] Reg 72 JSA Regs

[41] S 19(5) (a) & (10) (b)

[42] S 19(5) (b) (ii)

[43] Reg 73(2) JSA Regs

3 Income Support

What is Income Support?

Income Support is a means-tested benefit for people who are not working for 16 hours or more a week.

Who is entitled to Income Support?

You can receive Income Support if you are

- aged 16 or over
- not in full-time, non-advanced education (though there are exceptions), and
- not working 16 or more hours a week (there are a few exceptions), and, if you have a partner, they must not be working for 24 or more hours a week.

You must be in a particular group in order to be eligible for Income Support. The most common of these are:[1]

- unable to work because of ill health or a disability.
- caring for a disabled person who has claimed or who receives Disability Living Allowance or Attendance Allowance
- a lone parent responsible for looking after a child aged under 16
- maternity, adoption or paternity.

Education and training

You may receive Income Support while in full time education or training if you:

- are aged under 20 and at school or in full-time non-advanced education (i.e. up to A-Level or equivalent) and you have a disability which qualifies you for a benefit
- are deaf and you receive a disabled student's allowance
- have been granted refugee status and are attending an English course for over 15 hours a week during your first year in the UK
- are under 20 and in full-time non-advanced education and of necessity you have to live away from your parents or anyone acting in their place because of various reasons
- are aged 24 or younger and attending a course provided by the Learning and Skills Council, or its equivalent in Wales or Scotland.

Carers

You may receive Income Support as a carer if you are:

- Regularly and substantially caring for another person and either you receive Carer's Allowance, or the person you are caring for is receiving Attendance Allowance, or the middle or higher rate of Disability Living Allowance care component or constant attendance allowance paid under the Industrial Disablement Benefit or War Disablement Pension rules
- Caring for another person who has applied for one of the above benefits, but the claim has not yet been processed. You will be able to claim Income Support for up to 26 weeks while you are waiting
- Looking after a member of your family who is temporarily ill, as long as they are part of your assessment unit for Income Support purpose.

Caring for a child or children

You may receive Income Support as a carer for children if you:

- are a lone parent and responsible for a child under 16
- are a lone parent or a member of a couple and you have to take unpaid statutory parental leave to look after a dependent child, and you are entitled to Housing or Council Tax Benefit, Working Tax Credit with a disability or a severe disability element, or Child Tax Credit at a rate above the family element
- are single or a lone parent and are fostering a child under 16 through a local authority or a voluntary organisation
- are looking after a child under 16 because the child's usual guardian is ill or temporarily away or
- your partner is temporarily abroad and you are responsible for a dependent child.

Maternity, adoption and paternity

You may receive Income Support if you:

- or your partner are expecting a baby. You can claim Income Support from 11 weeks before the baby is expected until 15 weeks after it is born
- are taking paternity or adoption leave.

Other

You may receive Income Support if you:

- You qualify for Income Support urgent case payments as a person subject to immigration control.
- You have started work and are eligible for the first four weeks of Mortgage Interest Run-on.
- You are required to attend court as a Justice of the Peace, juror, witness, defendant or plaintiff.
- You are remanded in custody for trial or sentencing (you can only receive certain help with housing costs).
- You may be able to claim if you are involved in a trade dispute.

If you work more than 16 hours a week, you may be eligible for Income Support if you fall into one of the eligible groups listed above, as well as if you are:

- mentally or physically disabled and your hours or earnings are 75% or less than that of a person without your disability in the same job
- living in a care home and working (require personal care because of disablement, past or present dependence on alcohol or drugs, past or present mental disorder or terminal illness)
- a volunteer or working for a charity or voluntary organisation and only receive expenses
- regularly and substantially caring for another person
- a foster parent and paid by a health body, local authority or voluntary organisations to provide respite care in your own home·
- a childminder working in your own home
- a training course and receiving a training allowance
- involved in a trade dispute, but you are not working during the first seven days after the day you stopped work
- working more than 16 but under 24 hours and are still covered by the transitional protection you were awarded in 1991
- on statutory maternity, paternity or adoption leave

This is not an exhaustive list.

How is Income Support calculated?

Earnings

Income Support is a means-tested benefit so your earnings will be taken into account when calculating your eligibility.

Earnings do not include:

- payments in kind
- periodic payments, e.g. because employment has ended through redundancy

- payments made when an employee is on maternity leave
- sick pay
- occupational pensions
- payments of expenses for doing your job for example, specialist clothing, travel expenses, or telephone calls made entirely for work purposes.

As well as these, between £5 and £20 of your earnings is ignored, depending on which group you fit into.

Other income

Almost all other income is counted, but some is ignored. For example, these are ignored: Disability Living Allowance, Attendance Allowance, Child Benefit (if you also receive Child Tax Credit, Guardian's Allowance), children's earnings, payments in kind, payments made for you to a third party (unless for everyday food, fuel, clothing and some housing), volunteers' expenses, Education Maintenance Allowances, fostering allowances, voluntary and charitable payments.[2] If in doubt, seek advice.

If you receive Child Tax Credit, this is ignored along with your Child Benefit, but the Income Support calculation will not then take account of any children that you have.

Capital

You must have less than £16,000 in capital or savings unless you live permanently in a residential care home. If you have been between £6000 and £16,000 capital, you will be counted as having £1 income for each £250 (or part thereof) between these limits.

If you have capital assets outside the United Kingdom, these will count as capital for Income Support. If your capital (including property which you or your partner own) is in a country where you are not allowed to transfer the capital to the UK, you will be counted as having capital at its market value in that country. If you can transfer the capital (or proceeds of sale) to the UK, you will be counted as having capital to the value of what it is worth in the UK. In both cases, ten percent is taken off the value to allow for the cost of sale and/or transfer.[3]

If you deliberately get rid of capital to bring your capital down to the level where you can receive extra benefit, you can still be counted as having it and the DWP are allowed to infer an intention from unusually high, one-off expenditure.[4] Seek advice if you are unsure about this or if you are affected by it.

The applicable amount

This is the minimum amount the government sets down that you need to live on. It is normally increased each April. It is made up of a weekly personal allowance for you and your partner and weekly premiums (paid if you are disabled or a carer or bereaved) plus housing costs for things such as interest on mortgages and loans for repairs and improvement and service charges. If you pay rent, this is not included and you should claim Housing Benefit instead. This also means that your applicable amount may vary to take account of some of your circumstances.

If your income is less than your applicable amount, you will normally receive Income Support to bring your income up to the level of your applicable amount.

Some people with children do not receive Child Tax Credit, but receive Income Support calculated to include amounts for children. The government currently plans to move all people in this situation onto Child Tax Credit during 2008. Most people will see no difference in the amount of money they receive, some will gain and a few will lose. Get advice if you are affected by this.

The Work Focused Interview

When you claim Income Support, you will usually be asked to attend a Work Focused Interview unless an interview would not be appropriate or would not be of assistance. If you do not attend the interview without good cause, your claim will lapse. You can appeal if you think you had a good reason for not attending.

Endnotes

[1]   Schedule 1B Income Support (General) Regulations 1987

[2]   Schedule 9 Income Support (General) Regulations 1987

[3]   Regulation 50 Income Support (General) Regulations 1987

[4]   Regulation 51 Income Support (General) Regulations 1987

4 Benefits for people unable to work through disability/ill health

People whose illnesses or disabilities mean that they are unable to work ('incapable of work') should be able to receive one or more of the following benefits – the benefit they receive will normally depend upon whether they are employed, have paid National Insurance contributions or fulfil certain other conditions. You may also be able to receive Income Support and other means-tested benefits, either to top up these benefits, or as an alternative source of income if you don't meet the conditions of entitlement.

- Statutory Sick Pay (SSP)
- Incapacity Benefit (IB)
- Severe Disablement Allowance (SDA)

Statutory Sick Pay

This is a social security benefit which is paid by employers, for a maximum of 28 weeks, to employees who are too ill to work. It may be paid in addition to any occupational sick pay scheme that an employer has (people sometimes confuse the two).

Incapacity Benefit (IB)

This is paid by the Department for Work and Pensions to people who have enough National Insurance contributions (unless you qualify under the special rules for young people). Contributions paid by both employed and self-employed people count, as do some National Insurance credits.

Invalidity Benefit

This was abolished in April 1995 but some people who have received it continually since before its abolition may be receiving higher amounts of Incapacity Benefit.

Severe Disablement Allowance

This non-contributory benefit was abolished in April 2001 but if you were already receiving it before 6th April 2001, you may continue to receive it provided that you satisfy the old conditions of entitlement for this benefit. The same 'linking period' rules for IB apply (i.e. normally eight weeks but in some cases, two years).

Changes to benefits in 2008

The government plans to introduce major changes in October 2008 to benefits for people who are unable to work because of a sickness or disability. At the date of preparing this handbook, the proposals are still being developed. Full details will be included in the next edition. Under the proposals, current claimants will continue to be subject to the benefit regime described in this chapter. Once the proposed regulations come into effect, new claimants will be subject to the new regime.

Statutory Sick Pay (SSP)[1]

SSP is paid by employers to their employees. It is not means-tested and counts as income for means-tested benefits. It is payable for a maximum of 28 weeks. It is not paid for the first three days of any period of absence (unless the person has been on SSP within the last eight weeks). Occupational sick pay may last for more than 28 weeks when SSP stops. Some employers with high sickness rates may reclaim their spending on SSP from HM Revenue and Customs.[2]

Who is entitled to Statutory Sick Pay?

To qualify for SSP you must:

- have average gross earnings more than the lower earnings limit for National Insurance (£87pw)
- be incapable of work
- have been incapable of work for at least four days (unless you have been ill within the previous eight weeks)
- be within a 'period of entitlement', and
- have notified your employer.

(Note: before April 2006, there was an upper age limit of 65 to qualify for SSP.)

SSP is only paid for days that are normally worked ('qualifying days').[3] There are special rules where normal working patterns vary and advice may be needed.

Who is an 'employee'?

An employee[4] includes people employed by an employment agency, certain office holders and people on temporary contracts. It is not necessary to have a written contract of employment. Generally, whoever deducts National Insurance for the employee will be an employer.

Attempts by some employers to circumvent employees' rights by classing them as self-employed or as sub-contractors may be challengeable and specialist employment law advice should be sought in such cases.[5]

There are no minimum hours of work needed to qualify for SSP and it is possible to receive SSP from more than one employer (for example, if you have two part-time jobs). It is also possible to be unfit for one employment but fit for another and so receive both SSP and earnings from the other job.

Notification

Notification of sickness should be made in a form agreed with the employer and as soon as possible.

For the first seven days of sickness you should self-certify your sickness. After that, a medical certificate (Med 3, or a Med 5 if it is retrospective) should be provided. Medical evidence for SSP and Incapacity Benefit can also be provided by people other than a doctor – for example, a community nurse, physiotherapist or social worker, if it is reasonable in the circumstances (e.g. the person doesn't have a GP).[6] Additional evidence from other professionals may also help in borderline or unusual situations.

An employer who dismisses an employee solely or mainly to avoid paying SSP remains liable for paying SSP during the period of entitlement, or until the contract of employment, was due to end.[7] It may also be unfair dismissal and/or discrimination, and specialist employment law advice should be obtained. It is also worth involving the HM Revenue and Customs (HMRC) (who can enforce SSP) in any cases of failure to pay SSP.

After 28 weeks' SSP, the employer is legally required to send you a notice (SSP1) telling you that you have had the maximum amount of SSP.[8] You should then complete the SSP1 with details of your incapacity for work and send it and a medical certificate to Jobcentre Plus who will use it as a claim for Incapacity Benefit at the higher short-term rate, linking to the period on SSP. The SSP1 must also be sent if an employee is not entitled to SSP from the outset, so that he/she can use it to claim lower short-term rate Incapacity Benefit. If an employer fails to keep adequate records or fails to correctly notify an employee about their SSP, HMRC can make them pay a financial penalty of up to £300 plus a daily penalty and up to £3000 in more serious cases.[9]

If your employer refuses to pay SSP you can ask HMRC to make a decision[10] which then binds the employer, and which you can also appeal against if you feel it is wrong.

Incapacity Benefit

Incapacity Benefit is payable if you:

* have paid or been credited with enough National Insurance Contributions

and

* are accepted as being 'incapable of work' at the time you claim.

Some people aged between 16 and 25 may be able to receive Incapacity Benefit even if they don't have enough National Insurance contributions and even if they are still in full time education.[11] (see page 77) However, if a young person is living with parents/carers who receive Child Benefit and Child Tax Credit for the young person, seek advice before claiming IB for a young person because a successful claim can affect the parents/carers' benefits and tax credits.

There are three rates of Incapacity Benefit:

Short-term Incapacity Benefit at the lower rate

This is the equivalent of the old Sickness Benefit and is paid for the first 28 weeks' incapacity if you don't qualify for Statutory Sick Pay from an employer. It is tax-free.

Short-term Incapacity Benefit at the higher rate

This is paid from 29-52 weeks' incapacity if you have either received the lower rate, or Statutory Sick Pay (or a combination of these). It is taxable.

Long-term Incapacity Benefit

This is the equivalent of the old Invalidity Benefit and is paid from 53 weeks incapacity onwards to people who have received the short-term higher rate, or from 29 weeks to people receiving the higher care component of Disability Living Allowance or who are terminally ill. This is taxable.

The following additions can be paid with the basic benefit:

Age allowances (paid with long term rate only)

There are two age additions, depending on the age at which your period of incapacity for work first began:

Incapacity began before age 35: Higher age allowance

Incapacity began between 35 and 45: Lower age allowance

Some people who were on Invalidity Benefit before it was abolished on 13th April 1995, may receive different age allowances.

Young people

If you are aged over 16 but under 20, you may receive Incapacity Benefit without National Insurance contributions, if your incapacity began before your 20th birthday and if you have also been incapable of work continually for at least 28 weeks (which may be from before your 16th birthday).

If you are aged from 20 up to 25, you can qualify for Incapacity Benefit without contributions if you have been incapable of work for at least 28 weeks and:

- you were on an education or training course for at least three months before you were 20 and
- you have now left that course and
- the course ended within the previous two tax years before the calendar year and
- you claim before your 25th birthday.

Adult dependants

An addition for an adult dependant may only be paid if you have a spouse (i.e a married or Registered Civil Partner) who is aged over 60 or it is not your spouse and they care for your children.

If you are entitled to one of the short-term rates, or are claiming for a dependant you are not living with but you maintain them financially, the dependency addition is not paid if their net earnings are greater than the amount of the addition.

If you qualify for the long-term rate of Incapacity Benefit, the addition is not paid if the dependant's net weekly earnings exceed £59.15 net per week.

Child dependants

If you claimed Incapacity Benefit or Severe Disablement Allowance before 7th April 2003 and you qualify for a child dependency addition, you will continue to receive it until this element is eventually transferred to Child Tax Credit.

Linking rules

Breaks in benefit will be linked if you claim again within eight benefit weeks. This means that you don't have to re-do the waiting days nor receive the lower rates for another eight weeks before receiving the higher rate (the same rules apply to Statutory Sick Pay).

Breaks in IB of up to 104 weeks are possible if you enter employment or government funded work-based training for at least 16 hours a week, after receiving the long-term rate of Incapacity Benefit.

How to claim

Claim using the Incapacity Benefit claim pack (SC1) available from local Jobcentre Plus offices (or IB1(Y) form if claiming under the non-contributory rules for those under 25). A medical certificate is not required for the first seven days of incapacity, after which a medical certificate (Med 3 or Med 5 as appropriate or other evidence as described earlier) must be sent to the office handling the claim.

If you work for an employer and do not qualify for Statutory Sick Pay (for example, you do not earn enough to qualify), or you come to the end of your SSP (or you have left work), you need to send in the SSP1 claim pack which your employer sends to you.

Claims can be backdated for up to three months provided that evidence (e.g. a Med 5) is produced and the conditions of entitlement to Incapacity Benefit are met.[12]

In Jobcentre Plus areas, everyone must attend a work focused interview when they first claim IB, SDA or IS (on incapacity grounds) unless they are exempted because an interview would 'not be of assistance or would not be appropriate'). Failure to attend the interview without 'good cause' means that the claim is not processed.

People who live in the pilot Pathways to Work areas[13] will also be asked to attend regular interviews after the first eight weeks of incapacity for work unless they are exempt from the Personal Capability Assessment. Non-attendance without good cause will result in a cut in benefit payments. A special medical report about your capacity will also be compiled if you have a medical examination and will be forwarded to the personal adviser who interviews you at the Jobcentre. This will help the advisers and you agree an Action Plan for which you can receive a £20 a week 'job preparation premium' for carrying out tasks in the action plan and if you do return to work and earn less than £15,000 a year, you can receive a 'return to work credit' of £40 a week for 52 weeks. The government is going to gradually extend the Pathways pilot areas until they cover the whole country by 2008. You can be exempted from the interviews and other requirements if you are exempt from the Personal Capability Assessment.

Incapacity for work – what it means

Incapacity for work is decided according to legislation and there are two tests of incapacity. You do not need to be permanently incapacitated to qualify and if you qualify for Incapacity Benefit it does not mean that you are permanently incapable of work – which is one reason why your case may be regularly reviewed. You must also have a 'specific disease or bodily or mental disablement'.[14]

The 'own occupation' test and the Personal Capability Assessment

The Own Occupation Test

- Are you incapable of doing the work which you were reasonably expected to do in your job before falling sick?

The own occupation test applies for the first 28 weeks of the claim and if you have undertaken paid work of 16 hours or more a week for more than eight weeks in the 21 weeks before the date of claim.[15] If you haven't worked for this period (for example, you are unemployed), then the 'Personal Capability Assessment' test will apply from the start of your claim.

The Personal Capability Assessment

The PCA is an assessment of your ability to perform a range of everyday activities (but these should not be tested as if they are to be done in a work setting). The test is 'objective' – actual ability to do real jobs is not considered and non-medical factors such as age, qualifications, education and past work experience are not relevant. It is often based on an examination and questioning by a doctor contracted to work for the DWP's Medical Services, usually after ten weeks' incapacity.

There are two parts to the PCA:

- a physical assessment, and
- a mental assessment

For each assessment there is a list of 'descriptors'. These are statements describing your level of disability and you are asked to rate your ability against the descriptors. Points are then allocated to the different descriptors and incapacity for work is then decided on the number of points scored. (See page 262 for all the descriptors).

To be treated as incapable of work, you must score a total of either:[16]

- 15 points from the physical abilities list or
- 10 points from the mental abilities list or
- 15 points if you have a combination of physical and mental incapacity.

If you have a combination of mental and physical disabilities and you score between six and nine (inclusive) in the mental disability list, then a score of nine is added to the physical test. Scores of less than six are ignored.

In the physical abilities list you can only be awarded points for either walking or using stairs – not both: the highest score that they qualify for is awarded. For all other activities in the physical test, the highest score for each descriptor is awarded.

For the mental abilities test you are awarded points for each of the descriptors which apply. This means that up to nine points may be awarded for each activity.

The PCA acts as the gateway to benefit. In addition, when you attend a medical examination as part of your assessment, you may be asked for additional information about what you can do in spite of your illness or disability, and the way you move, undress and come across during the examination will also be observed. This information forms a Capability Report which may be used to give advice and support to sick and disabled people with a view to helping them get back to work, and in Pathways to Work areas, Jobcentre Plus Personal Advisers will be sent a copy.

More about the rules of entitlement

When the own occupation test applies, you send in medical certificates signed by your doctor.

When the Personal Capability Assessment applies benefit continues to be paid whilst the PCA is being undertaken. Med 3 certificates should continue to be supplied until Jobcentre Plus notifies you otherwise.

If the Med 3 has identified a condition which may result in exemption (including mental health problems or a learning disability), Jobcentre Plus will contact your doctor to enquire about the severity of it. If exempted, Jobcentre Plus will notify you and your doctor. No further medical certificates need be supplied and you will not have to undertake the PCA.

Everyone who is not exempt is sent a questionnaire ('IB50') to complete which forms part of the decision about the PCA score. The IB50 contains questions about your physical limitations in the functional areas (although a small section of the form also asks about 'anxiety, depression and other mental health problems'). It is very important to complete this comprehensively and it is worth having help from a welfare rights adviser.

Failure to return the IB50 without good cause within six weeks[17] may result in your being found capable of work, and your benefit will then be stopped (Jobcentre Plus should send reminders before doing this). See page 18 for information about Jobseeker's Allowance. It is very important to appeal if benefit is stopped and appeals have a very high success rate – particularly if you are represented at the appeal by a benefits expert.

Following the return of the IB50, the Decision Maker at Jobcentre Plus will decide whether there is a need for a medical examination. Everyone with a mental health issue will be referred for a medical examination (unless they fall into an exemption category).

With mental health assessments, the DWP's doctor must be satisfied that the effects arise from a diagnosed psychiatric problem. If the condition is undiagnosed, the PCA will be applied and if it confirms a mental health problem, further information will be sought from the person's own doctor (which could be either their GP or a consultant).

The examining doctor then sends a report to the Decision Maker with advice on incapacity. A DWP Decision Maker decides entitlement to benefits for incapacity for work.

Exemptions

You may be accepted as being incapable of work and then won't have to undergo the PCA .[18]

You can be treated as incapable of work for any day when you are:

- a hospital in-patient
- under observation because of contact with, or suspicion of being a carrier of, an infectious or contagious disease and you have been excluded from work by a certificate from a Medical Officer for Environmental Health
- receiving particular treatment, for example, radiotherapy, chemotherapy, weekly renal dialysis
- pregnant, where there is a risk to health or safety of the mother or baby, or for a period six weeks before and two weeks after the birth
- terminally ill (death can be reasonably expected within six months)
- receiving the highest rate care component of Disability Living Allowance
- accepted as 80% disabled for the purposes of Severe Disablement Allowance or Industrial Disablement Benefit
- registered as blind.

You can also be treated as incapable of work even though you have scored insufficient points on the PCA to be classed as incapable of work, if there would be a risk to you or anyone else if you were found capable of work.

You may also be exempted if you have one of the following medical conditions:

- dementia
- tetraplegia
- persistent vegetative state
- paraplegia or uncontrolled involuntary movements or ataxia which effectively make you paraplegic

or, where there is medical evidence that you have one of the following conditions:

- severe learning difficulties (defined as 'arrested or incomplete physical development of the brain, or severe damage to the brain, which involves severe impairment of intelligence and social functioning').

- 'a severe mental illness involving the presence of mental disease, which severely and adversely affects a person' s mood or behaviour, and which severely restricts his social functioning, or his awareness of his immediate environment'.

- a severe and progressive neurological or muscle wasting disease.

- an active and progressive form of inflammatory polyarthritis.

- a progressive impairment of cardio-respiratory function which severely and persistently limits effort tolerance.

- dense paralysis of upper limb, trunk and lower limb on one side.

- multiple effects of impairment of function of the brain or nervous system causing severe and irreversible motor, sensory and intellectual deficits.

- manifestations of severe and progressive immune deficiency states characterised by severe constitutional disease or opportunistic infections or tumour formation (e.g. AIDS).

If a certificate of exemption is issued, you and your doctor will be notified and you will not have to provide medical certificates unless the claim is reviewed.

Important points

- If you have failed the PCA, you may need further medical evidence to support your incapacity for work. GPs and others can continue to provide medical certificates (and other evidence) in support of this. If you make a new claim for Incapacity Benefit within six months of being found capable of work, you will still be found capable of work unless your health has worsened or a new illness/disability has been diagnosed, or you were treated as capable of work solely because you failed to return the IB50 questionnaire.[19]

- People with a mental illness or learning disability may fail to return the IB50 because they don't feel it is relevant to them. They will need support or encouragement to understand the relevance and importance of this form and it is important that doctors give detailed information about the severity of the person's condition.
- When completing an IB50 it may be useful to refer to the PCA descriptors (see page 262).
- There have been many public concerns about the quality of work by the doctors contracted to the DWP and so it is prudent not to rely on their findings alone if a claim for Incapacity Benefit has been refused.
- While Incapacity Benefit is not means-tested, if you have an occupational or personal pension, half of the pension above £85 a week is deducted from your Incapacity Benefit. So if you have an occupational pension of £100 a week your Incapacity Benefit will be reduced by £7.50.
- If you are over pension age (65 for men, 60 for women), you can't receive the long term rate of Incapacity Benefit but the age addition may continue.

Working while on benefits

You can continue to be treated as incapable of work and continue to receive Incapacity Benefit, Severe Disablement Allowance and/or Income Support on the grounds of incapacity for work, if you do work which is:

- voluntary work, or
- permitted work, or
- an approved, unpaid work trial agreed in writing by Jobcentre Plus, or
- work as a councillor or as a 'disability member' of a Tribunal.

Voluntary work

A volunteer is someone who is: 'involved in voluntary work, other than for a close relative, where the only payment received by him or due to be paid to him... is in respect of any expenses reasonably incurred in connection with that work'.[20]

A close relative is defined as: 'a parent, parent-in-law, son, son-in-law, daughter, daughter-in-law, step-parent, step-son, step-daughter, brother, sister or spouse of any of the preceding persons, or if that person is one of a couple, the other member of that couple'.[21]

Government policy is to encourage such voluntary work because it promotes people's health and well-being and may be a route back into employment. However, many people receiving Incapacity Benefit may be anxious that voluntary work will jeopardise their benefit, and experience shows that DWP staff think that you are capable of work if you do voluntary work, and so send you for a medical examination. It is therefore useful to tell Jobcentre Plus about the details of the voluntary work being done and your limitations, preferably before it starts. There is no limit on the hours of voluntary work you may do.[22]

Permitted work

To count as permitted work, the work must be for less than 16 hours week on average and:[23]

- pay, on average, no more than £86 a week in a 52 week period. You can have another 52-week period if you stop receiving IB, SDA (or other benefits for incapacity for work) for more than 8 weeks, or if it is 52 weeks since you last worked and earned this amount while on benefit

- the permitted work pays less than £20 per week or

- you are in 'supported permitted' work and supported by a public or voluntary body who help people with a disability to find work, which pays no more than £86 a week. There is no time limit on this work. This kind of arrangement is more suitable if you are not realistically capable of moving back into full-time work for the foreseeable future.

- you have been exempted from the PCA and work for less than 16 hours pw and earn up to £86 pw for long as you are exempt.

- is work done as part of your treatment on therapy while you are in a hospital in-patient or outpatient and pays less than £86 per week on average.

These higher earnings limits are linked to the National Minimum Wage and normally increase each October.

'Supported permitted' work must be work which is done with ongoing support or supervision from a professional caseworker (from a voluntary or public sector body, this might include: nursing staff, social workers, support workers or Connexions/Careers advisers). It includes work done under medical supervision in hospital as well as work in sheltered workshops and, more importantly, work in an ordinary paid job.

It is very important to notify Jobcentre Plus (ideally in writing) about any work and to explain why it should be treated as permitted work or supported permitted work.[24]

If you do work more than 16 hours a week, you should inform Jobcentre Plus because you will no longer qualify for Incapacity Benefit and if you notify them within one week of starting work, you will be treated as a Welfare to Work Beneficiary which qualifies you to have a two year linking period (i.e. you may return to Incapacity Benefit at the same rate you were receiving without having to progress through the various lower rates again).[25]

If you receive means-tested benefits such as Income Support or Housing/Council Tax Benefits these benefits are still bound by the lower earnings limits for these benefits (currently £20 a week). This lack of symmetry in the social security rules undermines the good intentions behind the permitted work rules and means that most people thinking of doing permitted work will need advice and help to work out the effect on their overall income and benefit and tax credit entitlement before they start work (preferably using a suitable benefits software package).

Endnotes

1   Ss151 – 155 & schs 11 & 12 Social Security Contributions and Benefits Act 1995 ('SSCB Act')

2   S 159A Social Security Contributions and Benefits Act 1992

3   S 154 Social Security Contributions and Benefits Act 1992 & Reg 5 Statutory Sick Pay (General) Regulations 1982

4   Reg 16 Statutory Sick Pay (General) Regulations 1982

5   S 151 Social Security Contributions and Benefits Act 1992

6   Reg 2(1)(d) Social Security (Medical Evidence) Regulations 1976

7   Reg 4 Statutory Sick Pay (General) Regulations 1982

8   Regs 15 & 16 Statutory Sick Pay (General) Regulations 1982

9   HMRC Employer helpsheet E14 supplement

10   S8 Social Security Contributions (Transfer of Functions etc) Act 1999

11   S30A (2A) Social Security Contributions and Benefits Act 1992

12   Reg 19(1) and sch 4 Social Security (Claims and Payments) Regulations 1987.

13   At the time of writing, these areas are: Derbyshire, Highlands, Islands, Clyde Coast and Grampian, South Wales Valleys, Lancashire, Dorset and Somerset, South and Tyne Wear Valley, Essex, Cumbria, Glasgow, Tees Valley, South Yorkshire, Lanarkshire and East Dunbartonshire, Liverpool and the Wirral, Greater Manchester Central, South West Wales, Greater Mersey, Staffordshire, Ayrshire, Dumfries, Galloway and Inverclyde, Northumbria. See page 230.

14   S171B(2) Social Security Contributions and Benefits Act 1992

15   S171B(1) Social Security Contributions and Benefits Act 1992 & reg 491) Social Security (Incapacity for Work) (General) Regulations 1995

16   Reg 25 (3) Social Security (Incapacity for Work) (General) Regulations 1995

17   Reg 7 Social Security (Incapacity for Work) (General) Regulations 1995

18   Regs 10 – 14 Social Security (Incapacity for Work) (General) Regulations 1995

19   Reg 28 (2) (b) Social Security (Incapacity for Work) (General) Regulations 1995

20   Reg 2 (1) Social Security (Incapacity for Work) (General) Regulations 1995

21   Reg 2 (1) Social Security (Incapacity for Work) (General) Regulations 1995

22   Reg 17 (1) (b) Social Security (Incapacity for Work) (General) Regulations 1995

23   Reg 17 Social Security (Incapacity for Work) (General) Regulations 1995

24   DWP: Memo DMG Vol 3 08/06. Para 11.

25 Reg 13A(1)(d)(i) Social Security (Incapacity for Work) (General) Regulations 1995

5 Help with housing costs

Housing Benefit

What is Housing Benefit?

Housing Benefit helps people on a low income to pay their rent.[1] It is a means-tested benefit which may be available if you pay rent on the home you live in. It does not matter what type of rent you pay and Housing Benefit can be paid to licensees or tenants.

Who is entitled to Housing Benefit?

You may qualify for Housing Benefit if:

- you are liable to pay rent on a home that you are occupying
- you are resident in Great Britain and not subject to an immigration restriction
- your capital is not more than £16,000 (unless you also receive the guarantee credit part of Pension Credit which has no capital limit)
- any savings over £6000 reduce the amount of weekly benefit you are entitled to.

The amount of Housing Benefit you get will depend on various factors including:

- whether you are liable to pay rent or other charge for your accommodation
- the amount of rent you are liable to pay
- your income and capital
- the number of people you are able to claim for.

It does not matter what type of rent you pay. If you are buying a share of your council or housing association home but still pay rent on the other part, you can get Housing Benefit towards the rent share and you may also be able to get Income Support or Income-Based Jobseeker's Allowance towards your mortgage interest on the other share.

The basis for working out your Housing Benefit is 'eligible rent'.

Not all your rent will be eligible to be met by Housing Benefit and some payments you make to your landlord are excluded. These include:

- some service charges
- charges for light and heating
- charges for water
- charges for meals.[2]

This applies whether you are in work or not.

How is Housing Benefit calculated?

Means test

You are only able to receive maximum Housing Benefit if:

- you receive Income Support
- you receive income-based Jobseeker's Allowance
- you receive the guarantee credit part of Pension Credit, or
- your income is below your applicable amount.

If none of the above applies, then the amount of Housing Benefit you qualify for will be gradually reduced, depending on your income, so that the higher your income is above the applicable amount, the less Housing Benefit you will be paid.

If your income is above the applicable amount then your Housing Benefit per week will be calculated as:

- your weekly eligible rent, minus
  - any amounts for non-dependants, minus
  - 65% of your excess income.

The excess income is the amount of your income above the applicable amount. In effect you lose 65p for every £1 you earn over your applicable amount. This means that if you receive Housing Benefit while in work and your pay increases, you will lose most of that increase as a result of your Housing Benefit reducing.

Who can you claim for?

You can include your partner (including a same-sex partner whom you live with as a couple), children under the age of 16 who live with you and young people aged 16-20 who live with you and who are either in full-time education (doing a course up to A level/Scottish Highers standard) or who are in unwaged training which is funded by the government.

Other people who live with you may be classed as 'non-dependants' which may affect the amount of Housing Benefit you receive.

Non-dependants

A non-dependant is someone who lives with you but is not considered part of your family for benefit purposes, for example a grown-up child who is no longer a dependant, a relative or a friend. Your Housing Benefit and/or Council Tax Benefit will be reduced if you have one or more non-dependants, because it is assumed that they contribute towards your rent and/or council tax.

The following are not classed as non-dependants:

- boarders, sub-tenants and joint tenants (i.e. they are also liable to pay rent to your landlord)
- certain types of carer provided by a charity

- children under 16 or aged 16-20 and in full time education or unwaged training
- a landlord and any of their family members.[3]

Even if you do have non-dependants living with you, there will be no non-dependant deduction if you or your partner:

- are registered as blind or ceased to be registered within the last 28 weeks
- receive the care component of disability living allowance (paid at any of the three rates)
- receive attendance allowance
- receive constant attendance allowance.[4]

Similarly, there will not be a deduction if the non-dependant:

- receives a training allowance as part of work-based training for young people
- is a full-time student (but only during their summer vacation and if they are not in work, unless you or your partner are aged 65 or older).
- is aged under 18
- is aged under 25 and receives Income Support or Income-Based Jobseeker's Allowance
- receives Pension Credit
- has been in hospital for more than 52 weeks
- is in prison or
- does not normally reside with you.[5]

Non-dependant deductions can be very high and errors are common. The deduction can also depend on whether the non-dependant is in full-time paid work and how much they earn. There are six bands of non-dependant deductions which are based on the non-dependant's earnings.

Who is entitled to help with rent?

Liability for rent

To be eligible to claim Housing Benefit:

- You must be liable to pay the rent or similar accommodation costs on your home[6] (a written agreement to make payments is not strictly necessary, but having a proper written agreement such as a tenancy or licence agreement will avoid problems as well as give you clearer housing rights)
- The home you are claiming Housing Benefit for must be the one you and your family normally occupy.

There are exceptions to these rules. You can get Housing Benefit while you live away from home as long as:[7]

- you do not live away from home or longer than 13 weeks and
    - you intend to return to your home
    - you do not sub-let the property.

If you stay away for more than 13 weeks you will lose all of your benefit, however there is no set rule for how long you have to return for.

It is also possible to get Housing Benefit for up to 52 weeks if:

- you are on a training course either in the U.K. or abroad
- you are a hospital in-patient
- you have health related problems (you will need to seek advice about this).

There are special rules about getting Housing Benefit when you move from one home to another:

- You can claim Housing Benefit up to 13 weeks before you are liable for the rent.[8]

- When you move from one rented home to another, in certain situations, you may get Housing Benefit on both homes for up to four weeks if you have actually moved into the new home but you are liable to pay rent on both homes, or 52 weeks if you have had to move because of a fear of violence.[9]

Seek advice if you think any of these circumstances apply to you.

Reductions in your eligible rent

Housing Benefit can be reduced if:

- your rent is deemed unreasonably expensive or your accommodation is unreasonably large.[10]
- you live in private accommodation, in which case the rent can be restricted to the average private rent for the area that you live in.[11]
- you live in a Standard Local Housing Allowance pilot area[12] and your rent is higher than the Allowance for the area.
- you are under 25 and living alone, in which case your rent may be restricted to the average level of the rent for a room in shared accommodation in the area.

If there is a chance that any of these rules apply to you, you should get further information or advice as there are many exceptions.

You can find out about the rent levels in your area paid by the local housing benefit authority by:

- formally asking for a pre-tenancy determination before you take on your tenancy which is for private sector tenancies only
- informally asking Housing Benefit officers or an advice centre about the levels of rents that are paid in the area.

The restrictions on rents do not apply to some people who have been claiming Housing Benefit from before 1 January 1996.

You can keep this protection if:

- you do not stop claiming Housing Benefit for more than 52 weeks
- you or your partner are:
  - incapable of work because of ill-health or disability or
  - responsible for a child or dependent young person.[13]

Other claimants are allowed to have a gap in housing benefit of no more than four weeks.

If you wish to remain exempt from the deduction it is best to seek advice and further information – especially if you are thinking of moving home.

Working and receiving Housing Benefit

If you start working full time then you may be able to get Housing Benefit at the rate paid to you whilst you were claiming Income Support or Income-based Jobseeker's Allowance or Incapacity Benefit or Severe Disablement Allowance for the first four weeks. This is known as Extended Housing Benefit (see page 255).

You do not need to make a new claim each time you return to work. You need only report any changes in your circumstances to the local authority or the DWP. Housing Benefit will then be paid at the previous out-of-work rate until the new benefit level is recalculated to take account of your work income, even if this goes beyond the four week run-on period. It is important to notify the local authority of changes in your circumstances, such as starting work or increasing your hours of work in order to qualify for an Extended Payment and to avoid being overpaid and action being taken against you as a result.

You may be able to work full time and receive Housing Benefit. The amount you get will depend on:

- your income and
- the applicable amount (see page 277)
- the amount of rent you have to pay.

Keep in mind that the rules for Housing Benefit are different for lone parents. Lone parents are allowed to earn £25 per week before your income is counted. Other people who are working are allowed to keep between £5 and £20 a week before earnings count as income, depending on their circumstances. You can also keep up to £15 a week in child maintenance before it is counted as income.

An additional £15.45 per week of earnings is disregarded for many tenants who work 16 or more hours a week (and others who work 30 or more hours a week).

You may also offset your childcare costs up to maximum of £175 a week for one child or £300 a week for up to two children if you:

- are a lone parent who works 16 or more hours a week
- are a couple and both of you work 16 or more hours a week or
- one of you works 16 or more hours a week and the other is unable to work because of ill health or disability or they receive a disability/ill health benefit.

The childcare must be for a child aged under 15 (16 if the child is disabled) and should also be formal childcare such as a registered childminder, nursery, after-school club or a registered childminder in your home.[14]

Training schemes and Housing Benefit

The general rules are that:

- The training allowance received by people on training schemes is not classed as earnings but will normally be treated in full as income (unless you or your partner are aged 60 or older).
- Reimbursed expenses for training (for example, travel or childcare costs) are ignored.[15]

New Deal and Housing Benefit

The New Deal and Housing Benefit rules are that:

- if you are on a New Deal scheme and you are employed then you will be treated as being in paid work
- if a Training Allowance is paid, this is taken fully into account unless you are treated as being a trainee (this is because the allowance includes an Income-Based Jobseeker's Allowance payment of 10 pence).

Any awards made by Jobcentre Plus are disregarded as capital for 52 weeks. The following are disregarded:

- training premiums
- any childcare costs that are reimbursed to a New Deal participant and
- if the childcare payment is made as a lump sum it should be disregarded as a notional or actual capital for 52 weeks.

Your Housing Benefit should not be affected if:

- you are in an Employment Zone and therefore receiving Income-Based Jobseeker's Allowance or
- you are on a paid work placement if it is a subsidised job.

The Employment Zone weekly payments are disregarded as income and any arrears will be treated as capital and disregarded for 52 weeks.

For youth trainees and youth trainee employees the rules are:

- if you are an employee, the normal earnings rules apply
- trainees receive a training allowance from which no tax or National Insurance contributions are deducted.

If you are a trainee, these allowances count as income other than earnings. However, you do not have to count any reimbursed travelling expenses or training premiums.

Council Tax Benefit

Council Tax Benefit helps people on a low income to pay their Council Tax. There are two types of Council Tax Benefit:

• Council Tax Benefit which is the main source of help
• Second adult rebate which is formally known as Alternative Maximum Council Tax Benefit.

You may qualify for either of these benefits if you are in full-time work, part-time work or if you are not working. You may be able to get help under the second adult rebate scheme if you are responsible for Council Tax, you are single (or your partner is not liable for Council Tax) and your income is too high for Council Tax Benefit, but there is someone living in your property who is on a low income or is claiming Income Support or Income-based Jobseeker's Allowance. You should get further advice.

Who is entitled to Council Tax Benefit ?

Council Tax Benefit is a means-tested benefit and the means test rules are the same as those for Housing Benefit.

People who are excluded from Council Tax Benefit are:

• individuals who are subject to immigration control or classed as a person from abroad and
• most full-time students.

Many of the rules for Council Tax Benefit are similar to those of Housing Benefit, so for example you can get Council Tax Benefit during a temporary absence from your home but you can only claim Council Tax Benefit on one home.

Council Tax Benefit restrictions

There are restrictions on the amount of help given with Council Tax Benefit. Apart from the means test itself the calculation is based on your weekly eligible Council Tax.

Council Tax Benefit is based on your Council Tax liability after you have been awarded any reduction in your Council Tax (for example, because of a disability reduction or for certain types of carer).

How is Council Tax Benefit calculated?

The way in which Council Tax Benefit is calculated is similar to Housing Benefit.

If your income is above the applicable amount your Council Tax Benefit is reduced by 20%. In other words, you lose 20 pence for every £1 you earn over your applicable amount.

Help with Council Tax costs

You can also reduce the cost of Council Tax charges by ensuring you are receiving any deductions applicable to you. Deduction might apply if:

- You are single: your Council Tax can be reduced by 25% if you live on your own.

- You have a disability which requires your home to be adapted or for a special room to be set aside for your needs. You might be able to have your Council Tax reduced into a different valuation band.

- An adult living in your home is a carer, a full time student, severely mentally impaired or in one of the other groups who are not liable for Council Tax.

You should get advice or ask at the Council Tax office.

Help with mortgages

There is limited help available with mortgage costs. You can only get help with mortgages if:

- you receive the guarantee credit part of Pension Credit or
- you receive Income Support or Income-based Jobseeker's Allowance
- your net income is below the applicable amount.

The help is only with interest (calculated using a standard interest rate) on a mortgage or loan for repairs and improvements up to £100,000. Capital, endowment and insurance payments are excluded. You can also receive help with the cost of service charges if you are a long leaseholder.

The amount of help you qualify for with mortgages and leasehold costs is included in the applicable amount calculation for Income Support, Income-based Jobseeker's Allowance or Pension Credit (see chapter 29). This means that if your income is otherwise too high for one the qualifying benefits above, you may qualify when your housing costs are included in your applicable amount calculation.

If you or your partner is aged under 60, you will usually have to wait for a period until you receive any help.

If you took out a loan or mortgage on or after 2 October 1995, you will not get any interest at all for the first 39 weeks of a claim. Even if you don't qualify, it is still important to make a claim so that the clock is started.

If you took out or loan or mortgage before 2 October 1995, you will receive nothing for the first eight weeks after a claim, then half the interest for the next 18 weeks and then full help after 26 weeks.

Some people who took out loans after this date can be given help under the more generous rules for loans before 2 October 1995. These are:

- lone parents who have been 'abandoned'
- carers receiving Carer's Allowance

- carers looking after someone who receives or who has claimed Attendance Allowance or higher or middle-rate Disability Living Allowance care component
- you are claiming while in prison awaiting trial or sentence
- you have a mortgage protection policy but you have been refused help on certain medical grounds.[16]

If you stop receiving Income Support, Income-based Jobseeker's Allowance or Pension Credit and you then have to claim again, there are rules which allow some people to be off for 12 weeks and others for 104 weeks without having to wait again until they receive help – these are known as linking periods. This is a very important thing to consider if you are thinking of taking a temporary job and you should get advice to see which linking period you qualify for.

Payment towards your mortgage interest is usually paid directly to your lender every four weeks. It is very important to discuss your circumstances with your lender if you have to claim Income Support, Income-based Jobseeker's Allowance or Pension Credit.

Your mortgage interest can be paid for up to four weeks when you start work (see page 255).

As with Housing Benefit, mortgage interest can be reduced in some cases if:

- the home is too big or too expensive
- you have non-dependants living with you
- the loan is for certain types of repairs and improvements which don't qualify.

If it is possible that any of these circumstances might apply to you, seek further advice and information.

Endnotes

[1] Housing Benefit Regulations 2006 ('HB Regs') & Housing Benefit (Persons who have obtained the qualifying age for State Pension Credit) Regulations 2006 ('HB(PC) Regs').

[2] Reg 12(3)(b) HB Regs & reg 12(3) HB(PC) Regs.

[3] Reg 3 HB Regs and reg 3 Council Tax Benefit Regulations 2006

[4] Regs 2(1) & 74(6) HB Regs & regs 2(1) & 55(6) HB(PC) regs

[5] Regs 2 (1) & 74 HB Regs & Regs 2(1) & 55 HB(PC) Regs

[6] Regs 11 & 13 HB Regs

[7] Reg 7 HB Regs

[8] Reg 83 HB Regs

[9] Reg 7 HB Regs

[10] Reg 12 HB Regs

[11] Reg 13(4) & (6) HB Regs

[12] These areas are: Argyll and Bute, Blackpool, Brighton and Hove, Conwy, Coventry, Eat Riding of Yorkshire, Edinburgh, Guildford, Leeds, London Borough of Lewisham, Northeast Lincolnshire, Norwich, Pembrokeshire, Salford, South Norfolk, St Helens, Teignbridge and London Borough of Wandsworth

[13] Sch 3 para 4(1) (a), (3) &(4) Housing Benefit and Council Tax Benefit (Consequential Provisions) Regulations 2006

[14] Regs 27(1) (c) & 28 (6) – (8) HB Regs

[15] Sch 5 para 13 HB Regs

[16] Sch 3 para 8(2) & (3) Income Support (General) Regulations 1987 & Sch 2 para 7(3) – (6) Jobseeker's Allowance Regulations 1996

6 Child Benefit

What is Child Benefit?

Child Benefit is a tax-free benefit for people who have a dependent child or children and 90% of those who are entitled to Child Benefit are also entitled to Child Tax Credit (see page 242).

Child Benefit is not based on your assets, income or savings and receiving Child Benefit does not reduce your entitlement to Working or Child Tax Credit.

Child Benefit is a very important benefit for people who go into work because it helps to reduce the poverty trap effect.

Dependent Children

A dependent child is defined as someone who is:[1]

- under the age of 16, or
- under the age of 20 (provided that education/training started before the age of 19) and also studying for A-levels, GNVQ level 3 or equivalent or undertaking unwaged training which is funded by the government,
  and
- studying for more than 12 hours a week at school or college (not including homework, private study, unsupervised study or meal breaks).

A child stops being dependent on you when they:

- get married
- get certain benefits in their own right (for example Income Support, income-based Jobseeker's Allowance, Incapacity Benefit)
- have employed trainee status
- are in custody
- are in care for more than eight weeks (unless they come home for at least two nights a week)
- are 16 and over and work for 24 hours or more a week.

Once any of these happen, you will no longer be entitled to Child Benefit and you should inform the Child Benefit office to avoid being overpaid.

The terminal date

If your child reaches 16 and they decide to leave school, your Child Benefit (and Child Tax Credit) will continue until the 'terminal date'. This is the last day of the following months after they leave education or training: August, November, February or May.[2] If they have not found a job after the terminal date, you can apply to have Child Benefit (and Child Tax Credit) paid for up to another 20 weeks from when the Child Benefit Extension Period starts, provided that they have registered with the Connexions/Careers Service.

Date of leaving education or unwaged training	Date Child Benefit stops ('terminal date')	Date Child Benefit Extension Period (CBEP) starts	Date Child Benefit Extension Period stops
December - February	Last day in February	First Monday after leaving	20 weeks after start of CBEP
March - May	Last day in May	First Monday after leaving	20 weeks after start of CBEP
June - August	Last day in August	First Monday after leaving	20 weeks after start of CBEP
September - November	Last day in November	First Monday after leaving	20 weeks after start of CBEP

If your child is going to stay in or return to education or training, you should inform the Child Benefit office (and the Tax Credit office) so that they can pay you.

Who receives Child Benefit?

The person responsible for the child should always make the claim. This person must normally be living with or supporting the child through maintenance. Child Benefit for an individual child (and other benefits and tax credits) can't be shared when a separated couple share care of one child, though if there is shared care for more than one child, the Child Benefit for each child may be shared by paying Child Benefit for each child to each parent.[3]

If you receive Child Benefit for a full tax year, for a child under 16, you are entitled to home responsibilities protection. This protects the amount of Retirement Pension and/or bereavement benefits you may be entitled to at a later date if your National Insurance contributions are affected because you are bringing up children and not able to earn enough in order to pay National Insurance contributions.

If your partner is working and paying National Insurance, but you are not, then make sure it is you who is claiming the Child Benefit if you have a child aged under 16. Home Responsibilities Protection for people who receive Child Benefit should happen automatically – you don't need to make a separate claim.[4]

Home Responsibilities Protection will not protect your rights to benefits such as Jobseeker's Allowance or Incapacity Benefit, so if you are unable to work because of unemployment or incapacity for work, you should consider claiming these in order to receive a full National Insurance contribution credit.

How to claim

You can claim online at www.direct.gov.uk or by phoning 0845 302 1444 (Great Britain) or 0845 603 2000 (Northern Ireland). Many parents of new babies receive a 'Bounty Pack' in hospital. This may contain a Child

Benefit claim form. You will also need to register the child's birth so that you can claim any benefits or tax credits for him or her.

There is no upper age limit for a parent or carer to qualify for Child Benefit.

You should register the birth and claim as soon as possible after the child is born, because Child Benefit can only be backdated three months from the date your claim is received.

How is Child Benefit calculated?

See page 278 for Child Benefit rates.

A higher award is made for the first child and a lower award for the second and every subsequent child. Lone parents only receive a higher payment for their first child if they started claiming Child Benefit before July 1998.

Child Trust Fund

What is it?

Child Trust Funds are designed to help children to build up savings which they can draw on when they reach the age of 18.

Each child born from 1 September 2002, will be given a voucher worth £250 by the government provided a Child Benefit claim has been made, (a separate claim for a Child Trust Fund Payment will not be required), and the child is living in the UK. Vouchers can then be paid into special accounts which cannot be touched until the child reaches 18.

Those entitled to maximum Child Tax Credit (i.e. they have an annual income which is less than £14,495) will receive £500.

All Child Trust Funds can be supplemented by annual payments of up to £1,200 by parents, family and friends. At the age of seven, the government will make a further payment. The value of a Child Trust Fund is ignored for any benefit or tax credit claims and will also be tax-free.

Endnotes

1   S142(2) Social Security Contributions and Benefits Act 1992 & regs 2-7 Child
    Benefit (General) Regulations 2006

2   Reg 7(2) Child Benefit (General) Regulations 2006

3   R v Board of Inland Revenue ex p Ford [2005] EWHC 1109. 19th May 2005.

4   Reg 2(5) The Social Security Pensions (Home Responsibilities) Regulations 1994

The Social Fund

What is the Social Fund ?

A one-off social security payment towards the cost of a particular need.

There are two parts to the Social Fund:

1. The regulated Social Fund – provides grants for expenses which arise for a specified reason: maternity expenses, funeral expenses, cold weather payments and winter fuel payments.

2. The discretionary Social Fund – provides grants and loans to meet a variety of other needs such as clothing or furniture.

You will have to meet the criteria, such as being in receipt of certain benefits. Obtaining help from the discretionary Social Fund is notoriously complex and perseverance is often essential.

The regulated Social Fund

Maternity Expenses[1]

You will be eligible to claim the Sure Start Maternity Grant, of up to £500 for each qualifying child, if:

- you have been awarded Income Support or income-based Jobseeker's Allowance, Working Tax Credit with a disability or severe disability element, or Child Tax Credit or Pension Credit which is paid at a rate which is higher than the family element of £545 a year, and
    - you or your partner are pregnant and within 11 weeks of giving

birth, or
- you or your partner have given birth in the last three months, or
- you have adopted a child under the age of one
- you have a Residence Order under the Children Act (or equivalent Scots or Northern Irish legislation) for a child under the age of one,[2] or
- you have been granted a parental order for a child born to a surrogate mother.

You must also have advice on the health of your baby from a healthcare professional.

Funeral Payment

You will be eligible to claim a Funeral Payment if:[3]

- you or your partner accept the responsibility for the costs of a funeral which takes place in the United Kingdom. If you are a worker from a European Economic Area (EEA) country or a family member of a worker or you have the right to reside in the UK under EC law, you may receive help with the cost of a funeral outside the UK but in an EEA country.[4]
- the deceased was ordinarily a resident in the UK at the time of death
- you or your partner have been awarded Income Support, Income-based Jobseeker's Allowance, Pension Credit, Working Tax Credit with a disability or a severe disability element, Child Tax Credit which is paid above the family element, Housing Benefit or Council Tax Benefit, and
- you claim within three months of the funeral.

Cold Weather Payment

You are eligible for the Cold Weather Payment if you:

- receive Income Support or Income-based Jobseeker's Allowance or Pension Credit and receive benefit or Child Tax Credit for a child aged under five
- are aged 60 or over, or
- receive a disability premium, including the disabled child premium.

Winter Fuel Payment[5]

The Winter Fuel Payment is for people aged 60 in the week of the third Monday in September. It is normally paid automatically to people who receive Retirement Pension during this qualifying week, and others need to make a claim. Payment is made between mid-November and Christmas.

The discretionary Social Fund

Community Care Grant

Community Care Grants are for those on Income Support or Income-based Jobseeker's Allowance or Pension Credit to meet costs, which will:

- help them live in the community after being in institutional care
- help to reduce the chance that they will go into institutional care
- ease exceptional pressure on them and their family
- help them to set up home as part of a programme of resettlement after an unsettled way of life
- allow someone to care for a prisoner on temporary release or
- help with certain travel expenses within the UK.[6]

Budgeting Loan

Budgeting Loans are interest-free loans to help people who have been on Income Support or Income-based Jobseeker's Allowance for 26 weeks or more to buy a specific item.

The loan should be for:

- furniture and household equipment
- clothing or footwear
- rent in advance and/or removal expenses for new accommodation
- improvement, maintenance and security of your home
- travel costs

- expenses for seeking or starting work
- hire purchase or other debts for the above.[7]

The maximum loan that can be awarded is £1,500 and there is a minimum of £100. In all cases, the loan should be repaid within 104 weeks. However, your local Jobcentre Plus will get it repaid by having up to 20% of your weekly benefit reduced. Because these loans reduce your income, you should always apply for a Community Care Grant instead if you feel you qualify.

If you need help with the costs of finding work or taking a job, you may qualify for a grant which you don't have to repay from the Adviser Discretion Fund (see page 249).

Crisis Loan

The Crisis Loan is an interest-free loan for people who are unable to meet a short-term need or who need money in an emergency or because of a disaster.[8]

To be eligible for a Crisis Loan:

- You must be aged 16 or over.
- The item you apply for must not be excluded from the Crisis Loan scheme.
- The amount awarded must not be more than you can afford to repay.
- You must need the loan because of an emergency.

and

- You must not have any other source of income or savings to cover the costs for which you are claiming the Crisis Loan. This includes your wages and the possibility of borrowing from your employer, but does not include Housing Benefit, other Social Fund payments, business assets, or personal possessions. Because these loans reduce your benefits, you should always apply for a Community Care Grant instead if you feel you qualify.

You can apply to have Social Fund loan repayments reduced and the Secretary of State has discretion to not recover. Seek advice if refused.

Endnotes

1 Reg 5(1) Social Fund Maternity and Funeral Expenses General Regulations 1987

2 Francis v Secretary of State for Work and Pensions [2005] EWCA Civ 13033

3 Reg 7 Social Fund Maternity and Funeral Expenses General Regulations 1987

4 Reg 7(1A) Social Fund Maternity and Funeral Expenses General Regulations 1987

5 Social Fund Winter Fuel Payment Regulations 2000

6 Direction 4 Social Fund Directions

7 Direction 2 Social Fund Directions

8 Direction 3 Social Fund Directions

7

8 Other benefits

This chapter briefly summarises some of the other benefits which you may be entitled to.

The other benefits included in this section are:

- Disability Living Allowance
- Attendance Allowance
- Carer's Allowance
- Benefits for work-related accidents and diseases
- Bereavement benefits
- Benefits for maternity and paternity
- Pension Credit
- Healthy Start.

Disability Living Allowance and Attendance Allowance

What are they?

Disability Living Allowance (DLA) is a benefit for people who first claim when aged under 65 who have a physical or mental disability (including mental illness, learning disability and behavioural problems). It can be awarded to children or adults. It is not means-tested, is tax-free and is paid on top of other social security benefits. It has two components, one for care and the other for mobility and there are three care component rates and two mobility component rates. It is paid to people who need help looking after themselves or who need someone on hand in case of danger and/or who find it difficult to walk or get around.

Attendance Allowance (AA) is the equivalent of the DLA middle or higher rate care component for people who first claim after age 65 but it is paid at two rates instead of three (there being no equivalent to the lower care component rate of DLA) and there is no mobility component.

Because it is based on your mobility needs and /or your needs for help or being watched over by someone else or because you can't do certain everyday personal tasks, DLA can be paid whether or not you are in work. Taking on a job or voluntary work while you receive DLA does not give the DWP legal grounds to look at your DLA award,[1] but in practice they often do look into your entitlement if you take on any work or increase your hours. This is because they assume that starting work may indicate that your disabilities have reduced.

DLA can help passport you onto higher amounts of benefits such as Working Tax Credit and Income Support.

Disability Living Allowance (DLA)

Who is entitled to Disability Living Allowance?

You must be aged:

- birth to 65 years for the care component
- three to 65 years for the mobility component (five years or over for the lower mobility component rate). If it is awarded, it can continue to be paid after the age of 65, provided that the person still meets the rules for receiving the benefit.

Also:

You must have needed help or had mobility problems for at least three months and the condition must also be likely to last for at least six months (unless you have a terminal illness).

Care component (3 rates)[2]

Lower rate

You must need attention in connection with your 'bodily functions' for a 'significant portion of the day', or (if aged 16 or over), must be unable to 'prepare a cooked meal' if you have the ingredients.

Middle rate

You must need 'frequent attention' in connection with your bodily functions from another person throughout the day or 'continual supervision to avoid substantial danger' to yourself or other people.

or

At night you need: 'frequent or prolonged attention' in connection with your 'bodily functions', or you need someone 'to be awake for a prolonged period or at frequent intervals for the purpose of watching over' you.

Higher rate

You must satisfy both the night and the day rules for the middle rate.

Mobility component (2 rates):[3]

Higher rate

You must be physically disabled and also one of the following:

- you are unable to walk or
- your ability to walk outdoors is so limited that you can only walk a limited distance, or at a slow speed or it takes a long time or you can only walk in an unusual manner so that you are 'virtually unable to walk' or
- the exertion involved in walking outdoors could affect your health or cause your health to deteriorate or
- you are both blind and deaf or
- you are severely mentally impaired with severe behavioural problems

and you also qualify for the high rate care component of DLA or

- you have had both legs amputated.

Lower rate

You must need 'guidance' or 'supervision' from another person most of the time in places that you are unfamiliar walking in. People with visual impairments or chronic anxiety problems can often qualify for this and you do not need to be physically disabled to qualify.

Children

As well as meeting the usual rules of entitlement children under 16 must also show that they have substantially more needs than other children in normal health. Quality and quantity of care are important. Children under 16 cannot use the 'cooking test' to receive the lower rate care component.

Publicly funded accommodation

If you live in certain types of publicly funded accommodation (e.g. local authority funded care or NHS hospital), it may affect your Disability Living Allowance.

Attendance Allowance (AA)

Who is entitled to Attendance Allowance ?

You must:

- be aged 65 or older
- show that you need help with personal care needs and/or supervision to avoid danger to yourself or others. The rules of entitlement are the same as the higher and middle rate care component of Disability Living Allowance.
- have needed help/supervision for at least six months (note: this is different from DLA).

How to claim

You can claim by phoning 0800 882200 and asking for a claim pack for AA or DLA to be sent to you. You can also print a claim form on the DWP website: www.dwp.gov.uk or claim online at: www.directgov.uk .It is not possible to backdate AA and DLA claims unless a claim is lost in the post, so it is important not to delay making a claim.

Further points

- You will not be called for a work-focused interview if you claim DLA on your own.
- It is important to complete the claim form as fully as possible as many claims are refused because people don't spell out their needs in detail.
- Entitlement is based on the help which is needed – not what is received.
- Help with things like ordinary gardening or housework won't normally qualify but in some cases, needing extra help with laundry (for example, because of soiling) may qualify.
- There is no set list of disabilities which qualifies – any type of long-term illness or disability may create needs which entitle you.
- If a claim is refused or you are awarded a rate that is too low, you have a good chance of success if you challenge this, but you should get independent advice.
- DLA can be kept if you are working.

Carer's Allowance (CA)

What is Carer's Allowance?

Carer's Allowance is a benefit for carers. It is not means-tested but entitlement can be affected by your earnings as there is a maximum amount you can earn if you receive it, (currently £87 net a week).

Carer's Allowance can increase entitlement to means-tested benefits because extra amounts for carers can be included in the calculation of these benefits.

Who is entitled to Carer's Allowance ?

You must:

- spend at least 35 hours a week looking after someone who receives either Attendance Allowance or the middle or higher care component of Disability Living Allowance
- not be in education which involves 21 or more hours' supervised study or teaching each week.[4]

If you are working part-time while receiving Carer's Allowance, you can offset certain expenses against your earnings when calculating whether or not your earnings are less than the earnings limit. The following can be offset from your gross earnings:

- Income Tax and National Insurance
- half of any contributions to a personal or occupational pension scheme
- the cost of paying a carer (who is not a close relative) to look after children or the person you care for while you are at work.
  Up to half your net earnings can be offset using these expenses.[5]

How to claim Carer's Allowance

You claim CA by completing form DS700, which you can get by phoning the DWP on 0800 882200 (textphone 0800 243355). You can also print a claim form from the DWP website. It is also possible to claim this benefit on-line at: www.directgov.uk .

Further points

- You can't receive CA if you also receive another non-means-tested benefit which pays the same as or more than your CA entitlement – for example, long-term rate Incapacity Benefit or Retirement Pension. However, you should still make a claim as this will give you underlying entitlement to CA which qualifies you for higher amounts of means-tested benefits.

- People receiving CA are also credited with National Insurance contributions.

- CA used to be known as Invalid Care Allowance, until April 2003, and people aged 65 or over were not entitled to newly claim it, before October 2002.

- If you claim CA you do not have to have a Work Focused Interview (see page 144) but you can choose to have one voluntarily. However, if you also claim another benefit such as Income Support or Incapacity Benefit, you will be required to have a Work Focused Interview.

- CA is awarded to a carer who cares for a named individual. This means that a couple can have two carers who receive CA.

- If a carer receives CA it may affect the means-tested benefits which the person they care for receives. Seek advice to check this before claiming.

- CA will be affected if the person being cared for enters hospital or publicly-funded care and their AA/DLA stops.

Benefits for work-related accidents and diseases

What are they?

There are a number of benefits for people whose ill health or disability is related to their employment. These are:

- Disablement Benefit
- Reduced Earnings Allowance
- Retirement Allowance and
- Constant Attendance Allowance.

They are often called industrial injury benefits and they are paid to people who have a disability or health problem which results from an accident at work or from a prescribed industrial disease. They are non-taxable, and non-contributory and they can be paid whether or not the person is working and regardless of their income or capital. They are also paid without the recipient having to prove negligence by the employer, or whether the employer has paid compensation. Because you can receive them while you are in work and because they don't reduce any tax credits you may qualify for, they are a useful welfare to work benefit.

Who is entitled?[6]

You must:

- be an employed earner (genuinely self-employed people are excluded)
- have had an accident arising out of and in the course of your work or be suffering from a prescribed industrial disease and have suffered a loss of faculty which has been assessed as a disability of at least 14% (1% for Reduced Earnings Allowance)
- have had the accident or contracted the prescribed disease at least 90 days before you claim and still have a disability/ill-health
- for Reduced Earnings Allowance, your accident or disease must have occurred before 10th October 1990 and you must be unable to follow your regular occupation or do work of an equivalent standard.

How to claim

You can get claim forms from a Jobcentre Plus office or print them from the DWP website: www.dwp.gov.uk/resourcecentre/claim_forms.asp.

Further points

- These benefits are not means-tested (though Reduced Earnings Allowance depends on the level of your earnings) but they do count as income for means-tested benefits. However, they are ignored as income for tax credits so they are particularly helpful if you are in work. They are not affected by the amount of any compensation for an injury but all benefits paid because of an injury may affect the amount of compensation you receive from legal action.
- You will not be asked to have a work focused interview if you make a claim.
- You will have to undergo a medical examination to assess the degree of your disability.

- Different amounts of Disablement Benefit are paid according to the degree of disability.

- It is important to register any accident or incident at work so that you have evidence if you later have to make a claim.

- People who are injured or contract a prescribed industrial disease while they are unwaged trainees on work-based training may be able to receive equivalent benefits under the Analogous Industrial Injuries Scheme. More information is available from 0800 590395 or at: www.dfes.gov.uk/aiisnet/idb.shtml.

- The full list of Prescribed Industrial Diseases is set out in Schedule 1 of the Social Security (Industrial Injuries) (Prescribed Diseases) Regulations 1985. It has been substantially amended over the years and there is a summary in the Welfare Benefits and Tax Credits Handbook published by Child Poverty Action Group.

Bereavement benefits

What are bereavement benefits ?

There are three benefits available for people who were legally married to or who had a Registered Civil Partnership with their partner at the time their death occurred. The benefits are contributory (payable at a lower rate if there are insufficient contributions) and count as income for means-tested benefits (but £300 a year of Widowed Mother's and Widowed Parent's Allowances are ignored for Tax Credits). It is not possible to receive a bereavement benefit and another contributory benefit at the same time – the overlapping benefit will usually be made up to the Bereavement Benefit level. Some bereavement benefits are taxable.

The three benefits are:

- Bereavement payment (one-off lump sum)

- Widowed Parent's Allowance (some people may still be receiving Widowed Mother's Allowance from before 9th April 2001) and

- Bereavement Allowance.

Who is entitled to bereavement benefits?[7]

Bereavement Payment – this is a tax-free lump sum of £2000 which does not count as capital for means-tested benefits. The surviving spouse/civil partner must be under pensionable age (60 for women, 65 for men) when the other spouse/civil partner dies. If the survivor is over pension age, a payment may still be possible if their late spouse/ civil partner was not receiving a Category A Retirement Pension. If the spouse/civil partner died from a work-related accident or a prescribed industrial disease, the National Insurance contribution conditions are waived. The Payment must normally be claimed within 12 months of a death – it is not paid automatically.

Widowed Parent's Allowance – this is for parents widowed on or after 9th April 2001. They must have dependent children (i.e. qualify for Child Benefit for at least one of them).

Bereavement Allowance – this taxable benefit is payable for 52 weeks from the date of the spouse/civil partner's death which must be on or after 9th April 2001. As one cannot receive both the Bereavement Allowance and the Widowed Parent's Allowance at the same time, it is effectively a benefit for people without dependent children. For people aged between 45 and 54 on the date that their late spouse/civil partner died, there is an additional age allowance payable. Bereavement Allowance is based on the late spouse's/civil partner's National Insurance record.

How to claim

All three benefits are claimed on a claim form from Jobcentre Plus offices, or by printing one from the DWP website: www.dwp.gov.uk/resourcecentre/claim_forms.asp .

Further points

- You will be asked to have a Work Focused Interview if you make a claim and you do not work for 16 or more hours a week, though this will normally be deferred for at least three months.

- These benefits are not payable to couples who never married or entered a civil partnership, and couples who have divorced (separation and not having a decree absolute, count as still being married) or where the civil partnership has been dissolved. However, occasionally long-standing relationships celebrated by a customary ceremony may qualify and in Scotland people can be classed as married if they do so by living together in a stable way over a long period of time.

- Women widowed before 9th April 2001 are covered by the old Widow's Pension and Widowed Mother's Allowance schemes.

- Bereavement Allowance and Widowed Parent's Allowance are both suspended if a widow/widower starts to live as a couple with another man or woman, or they remarry or enter another civil partnership. Bereavement Payment is not payable if the person claiming is living as a part of a couple at the time of claim.

- Surviving partners who receive Income Support, Income-based Jobseeker's Allowance, Pension Credit, Tax Credits with income below a set amount, Housing Benefit or Council Tax Benefit may qualify for a Social Fund payment toward funeral costs.

- DWP leaflet D49 What to do After a Death contains a lot of useful information. There is a separate version for Scotland.

- Financial help may be available from the deceased's occupational or personal pension scheme, trade union, or trade or professional body. It is worth establishing the deceased's work history to see if there is any help available from previous work or activities.

Benefits for maternity, adoption and paternity

What are they?

There are four benefits for maternity, adoption and paternity.

Women who stop work to have a baby may be able to claim:

- Statutory Maternity Pay, a social security benefit paid by employers for up to 39 weeks to women in employment who stop work to have a baby. This may be in conjunction with any employment-based maternity pay entitlement.

- Maternity Allowance, paid for up to 39 weeks to women who have worked continuously for 26 weeks out of the 66 weeks immediately before when the baby is due.
- Statutory Adoption Pay, paid for up to 39 weeks when a child under 18 is placed for adoption and the claimant has worked continuously for their employer for 26 weeks out of the 66 weeks immediately before when the baby is placed. Members of a couple can choose which one will take the Statutory Adoption Pay (and the leave entitlement which goes with it). Statutory Adoption Pay is paid at the same rate and in the same way as Statutory Maternity Pay.
- Statutory Paternity Pay for people (not just fathers) who take paternity leave for up to two weeks during the time they opt to take paternity leave within 56 days of the birth of a child. In the case of an adoption, members of a couple can choose who takes paternity leave, Statutory Paternity Pay and Statutory Adoption Pay.

Statutory Maternity Pay (SMP)

SMP is a weekly payment, paid by an employer, to women who stop work to have a baby. It is paid for up to 39 weeks and is taxable. It is not means-tested but counts as income for means-tested benefits. The first £100 a week of SMP is ignored as income for Tax Credits.

Who is entitled to Statutory Maternity Pay?

You must:

- be employed in the 15th week before the baby is due (the qualifying week)
- have worked for the same employer for at least 26 weeks by the qualifying week
- earn more than the National Insurance lower earnings limit (£87 per week).

SMP is paid at two rates. The higher rate (90% of previous eight weeks' average earnings before 16th week) is paid to all women who qualify and is paid for the first six weeks. The standard rate (£112.75 or 90% of average weekly earnings, whichever is less) is then paid for the next 33 weeks.

Women can choose to work up to the week when the baby is due and still be entitled to 39 weeks' SMP. And they are still entitled if they don't intend to return to work. The earliest date that SMP can begin is the 11th week before the baby is due. You can return to work for up to ten 'keeping in touch' days without it affecting your benefit.

How to claim

The employee must be given the form MAT B1. Their GP, clinic or midwife issues this to the woman at least 28 days before she intends to stop work and she should also ask her employer for SMP to be paid from when she stops work. For Statutory Adoption Pay, this time limit does not apply.

Maternity Allowance

Maternity Allowance is paid to women who have:

- worked as an employed or self-employed earner for 26 weeks out of the 66 weeks immediately before the week the baby is due
- average weekly earnings above the Maternity Allowance Threshold (£30) and
- are not entitled to Statutory Maternity Pay for the same week in respect of the same pregnancy.

It can be claimed from the 11th week before the week that the baby is due and is paid for 39 weeks. A standard rate of £112.75 a week is paid to women with average weekly earnings of £87 or more, if earnings average £30 - £86.99pw, 90% of average earnings is paid. You may work for up to ten 'keeping in touch' days without it affecting your benefit.

How to claim

Maternity Allowance is claimed on form MA1 from Jobcentre Plus offices or by printing this from the DWP website: www.dwp.gov.uk/resourcecentre/claim_forms.asp#m. This should be returned with the maternity certificate (MAT B1) at 26 weeks into the pregnancy.

Further points

- If you are not entitled to SMP, you should be sent form SMP1 by your employer which you can then use to claim Maternity Allowance. If you are not entitled to Maternity Allowance, Jobcentre Plus should automatically assess a claim for Incapacity Benefit with a view to awarding it from six weeks before the birth and for up to two after, provided that you have enough National Insurance contributions/credits. Medical evidence of incapacity for work is not needed in these circumstances.
- If you are not entitled to maternity-related benefits, you may qualify for Income Support on the grounds of pregnancy or illness and Income Support may also top up maternity benefits, provided that the conditions for Income Support are met.
- If Child Tax Credit is in payment, it can be increased as soon as a baby is born, rather than at the end of the award period. There are also additional amounts of Income Support, Housing Benefit and Council Tax Benefit payable for a baby who is under a year old.
- When you are on maternity leave, you are treated as if you are still in remunerative work if you or your partner makes a Tax Credit claim.

Pension Credit

What is Pension Credit?

Pension Credit (PC) is officially called State Pension Credit. It is a means-tested benefit for people aged 60 or older and it was introduced in October 2003.

There are two ways to qualify for Pension Credit – through the guarantee credit and through the savings credit.

Despite its name, Pension Credit has nothing to do with Tax Credits.

Who is entitled to Pension Credit?

You or your partner must:

- Be aged at least 60 to qualify through the guarantee credit
- Be aged at least 65 to qualify through the savings credit.

You (and your partner if you have one) must both:

- Have an income which is less than your appropriate amount for the guarantee credit and/or
- An income which is above the guarantee credit level but which still qualifies you for savings credit.

There is no capital limit, but if you have capital of more than £6000, you will be counted as having £1 a week income for each £500 above this. Certain types of income are ignored, the most common being Attendance Allowance, Disability Living Allowance, tax credits, Child Benefit, £10 of a War Pension and £5 - £20 of any earnings you may have.

Your appropriate amount is worked out as follows:

- £119.75 for a single person
- £181.70 for a couple, plus:
    - £48.45 if a single person or one of a couple is classed as severely disabled
    - £96.90 for a couple if both are classed as severely disabled
    - £27.15 for a carer
    - certain housing costs for owner occupiers (see page 90 of the section about housing support).

If your income is higher than the appropriate amount, you may receive Pension Credit through the savings credit on a tapering basis.

How to claim:

You can get a claim form by phoning the DWP's Pension Service on 0800 99 1234. They can also complete a claim form over the phone for you. You can also print off a claim form on the DWP Pension Service website: www.thepensionservice.gov.uk/pensioncredit/form.asp.

Further points:

- If you have been entitled in the past, your claim can be backdated for up to 12 months.

- If you or your partner are aged 65 or older, your PC award will usually last for up to five years (increased annually for inflation). You won't have to report many changes of circumstances such as an increase in capital or retirement income. You can ask for a re-assessment if your circumstances change – for example, if you are awarded Attendance Allowance which may increase the amount of PC you qualify for.

- Some people with capital above £16,000 can qualify for the guarantee credit. This will then passport them onto maximum Housing and Council Tax Benefits even though the capital limit for these is normally £16,000.

- There is no limit on the hours you may work if you receive PC (though some of your earnings may count as income in the means test).

- Part of PC is increased in line with average earnings rather than prices for the duration of the current Parliament. Retirement Pension increases in line with prices, which means that about another 100,000 people qualify each year.

Endnotes

1   See Social Security and Child Support Commissioners' decisions CSA/114/1990 and CDLA/2160/2003

2   S 72 Social Security Contributions and Benefits Act 1992 ('SSCB Act')

3   S 73 SSCB Act & reg 12 Social Security (Disability Living Allowance) Regulations 1991.

4   S70 SSCB Act

5   Reg 10(3) Social Security Benefit (Computation of Earnings) Regulations 1996

6   Ss 94 –120 SSCB Act

7   Ss 36-39 SSCB Act

8

9 Benefits decisions and appeals

Decision Makers

Decisions about benefit entitlement are made by Decision Makers in DWP offices.

Decisions about Tax Credits are made by Decision Makers who act on behalf of the Board of Her Majesty's Revenue and Customs, while decisions about Housing and Council Tax Benefits are made by staff who work for local authorities.

You are entitled to have a written explanation of the decision provided that you ask for one within one month of being sent the decision. The Decision Maker/local authority must then send you the explanation within 14 days.[1] You then have a further month after receiving the explanation, to take matters further. However, you do not have to ask for an explanation before challenging the decision.

Appeals

You are able to appeal against almost all decisions, such as:

- whether you are entitled to benefit
- how your benefit has been worked out
- whether your claim for Jobseeker's Allowance should be suspended or sanctioned and for how long.

However, you cannot appeal against decisions such as:

- whether or not the Government have set the right amounts of benefit to live on, and
- on what day of the week and how a benefit should be paid.

An appeal must be in writing and received by the office within one month of the date on which the decision was made[2] (which will be on the letter telling you the decision), not the date on which you received the decision. The appeal will then be forwarded to the Tribunals Service which administers the appeal tribunals. You should normally use form GL24 from the DWP (available on: www.dwp.gov.uk) to make your appeal.

If you appeal after the one-month date, you may still be able to get your case heard if you can show that

- there are reasonable prospects that the appeal will succeed *or*
- it is in the interests of justice for your appeal to be heard, and
- there are special circumstances which meant that it was not practicable for you to appeal within the normal time limit.[3]

You can also appeal about tax credits and Housing and Council Tax Benefits in the same way, as well as ask for a revision or supersession (see below).

Appeal Tribunal

The Appeal Tribunal is independent of the Department for Work and Pensions (DWP), the local authority and the HMRC, and is able to change decisions. It is normally made up of one legally qualified member who can ask others to also hear the appeal.

You do not have to attend if you would rather the decision was just made using documents. However, it is best to be there, as you can then clarify any facts that may not be clear from the documentation and you have a far better chance of winning your appeal if you do attend. And remember that you can take along someone to support you if you are not confident to go on your own. Ideally an adviser who understands social security law should represent you (for example, from an advice agency or a welfare rights service). Whatever you decide to do about representation, it is very important to get independent advice before the appeal hearing.

Some time after you have sent in your appeal letter, you will be sent a letter by the Tribunal Service asking whether or not you still wish to have your appeal go ahead. It is very important to reply to this letter because if you don't, your appeal may not proceed.

If you find there is a long delay in having your appeal case dealt with, you can ask the Regional Chairman of the Tribunal Service to issue a Direction to the DWP, local authority or HM Revenue and Customs to prepare their paperwork for the appeal to be heard quickly.[4]

If there is more than one member of the tribunal, they will try to reach a unanimous decision. If they cannot, the Chairman (who may be a woman) has the power to make the final decision. Any decision will usually be made on the day of the hearing. You will be told the decision verbally and then sent a short written summary later. You can also ask for a more detailed written decision.

Some travel costs to and from the appeal hearing will be paid. You may also be able to claim for loss of earnings or childminding costs. You must provide receipts for all expenses that you intend to claim.

Revisions

If you have no right of appeal against a decision, you can ask for the decision to be revised within one month of the date of the decision being sent to you (or a further 14 days after you have been sent a written explanation of reasons for the decision). You can also ask for a revision when you do have a right of appeal[5] and the DWP/HMRC/local authority should also consider revising a decision if you do send in an appeal.

If it is less than a month (or 14 days after being sent reasons) you do not have to give any reasons for asking for a revision. If it is more than this, but less than 13 months since the date of the decision, you will need to show that there are good reasons for applying late.[6]

It is also possible to ask for a benefit decision to be revised at any time (even years later) if there was an 'official error' (for example, the wrong amount of benefit was paid or some evidence was overlooked).[7]

A revision will normally take effect from the date of the decision being revised. The Secretary of State can also revise the decision at any time without a request from you. This may happen if, for example, a decision arose from an official error, or it was based on a mistake about any material fact.

Normally, you will have a right of appeal against a revised decision which is unfavourable.

Appeals against revisions

If a decision is not revised in your favour then, in most cases, you can appeal to a tribunal. You should appeal against the decision made by the Secretary of State within one month of the revised decision being made.

Supersessions

Supersessions are also a way that benefit decisions can be changed. However, a supersession will usually only take effect from the date that the request for a supersession is received[8] by the DWP, local authority or HMRC.

The main grounds for a supersession are:

- There has been a change of circumstances
- There was a mistake about or ignorance of a material fact
- A decision was wrong in law
- You have been awarded a benefit which affects your entitlement to other benefits (known as a 'qualifying benefit').

The Secretary of State can also supersede decisions and must do so in certain situations including:

- applying a sanction to your Jobseeker's Allowance
- stopping your benefit because it is felt that you are no longer incapable of work
- deciding that you have been overpaid a social security benefit

Appeals to Social Security Commissioners

Social Security Commissioners are judges who are independent of the DWP/LA/HMRC.

If you disagree with an appeal tribunal's decision on a point of law, you may be able to appeal to the Social Security Commissioner. It is very important to get independent advice before doing this – particularly if your case might set a bad precedent for similar cases.

To follow this course of action, you must apply to the tribunal chairperson in writing; see: www.tribunals.gov.uk for further details and advice.

Complaints

If you do not agree with the way in which a local council made a decision, you can also complain to the Council's Monitoring Officer and to the Local Government Ombudsman (www.lgo.org.uk). Before going to the Ombudsman, you will have to use the Council's internal complaints procedure.

If your complaint is against the Department for Work and Pensions, you can contact your Member of Parliament and ask them to take up your case and/or you can make a complaint through the Customer Services Manager for the office you are complaining about.

Endnotes

1 Reg 28 Social Security and Child Support (Decisions and Appeals Regulations 1999 ('D&A Regs')

2 Reg 31 D & A Regs

3 Reg 32 D & A Regs

4 Reg 38(2) D & A Regs

5 Reg 3 D & A Regs

6 Reg 4 D & A Regs

7 Reg 3(5)(a) D & A Regs

8 Regs 6 & 7 D & A Regs

10 Welfare to work programmes – an introduction

Jobcentre Plus has many programmes that are aimed at helping you get a job, and a number of these are detailed in the following chapters. These programmes have certain common features as well as differences, so this introduction covers the general aims. Some programmes - most of them major programmes aimed at large groups of people - are called 'New Deals'.

Jobcentre Plus operates under a 'Work First' philosophy. Programmes are tested according to whether or not they get participants into jobs quickly and cheaply. Programmes that do not succeed in getting people into jobs, and also those that are no better than others but higher cost, are ruthlessly discarded.

Jobcentre Plus' aim is any job that gets you off benefit – ideally full-time, but a job over 16 hours will enable you to claim Working Tax Credit and come off Jobcentre Plus benefits if you are a lone parent. The only qualification to the 'any job' aim is that work should be sustained – which means that you do not come back to claim benefits within three months.

A common feature is that Jobcentre Plus wants to help you to look for work yourself. Jobcentre Plus provides Personal Advisers who will in some cases help you apply for jobs, but more generally they will advise you what you need to do to make applications with a chance of succeeding.

Jobcentre Plus does recognise that there may be some people for whom paid work is not appropriate now. In these cases, the attempt is to help you so that when your circumstances change you are able to find work. Examples are when your children are old enough (although the definition of 'enough' changes – there is discussion that when pre-school and school-age childcare is available 8:00 a.m.-6:00 p.m. year-round, 'old enough' might drop to 8, 5 or 3). In a few cases Jobcentre Plus may recognise that work is not likely to be in prospect as far as can be seen.

In the early days of the New Deals, much emphasis was placed on training. This has recently reduced with evidence that training programmes have not often helped more people get into jobs (or stay in them) than programmes providing general work experience such as working in charity shops or cleaning up the environment. Often, the key point for employers is simply that you can show you are able to turn up where required (and on time) every day and work under direction. A reference showing that you can do this has proved, in many cases, to be as helpful as a qualification certificate in getting a job. Some would argue that such references are more useful than some qualification certificates.

In many Welfare to Work Programmes, some elements are provided by private or voluntary contractors. In all cases contractors will be paid extra if you get a job, and in many cases receive a further bonus if you both get a job and stay off benefit for three months. This is to make sure that contractors, as well as Jobcentre Plus staff, focus on how best to help you into work.

One common feature of welfare to work programmes is the Work Trial. Because this is a common feature, it is dealt with in this introduction rather than being repeated in each chapter dealing with individual programmes for which Work Trials may be available.

Part 2: Welfare to work programmes – Introduction to welfare to work programmes

WELFARE TO WORK HANDBOOK

141

Work Trials

Purpose of Work Trials

Work Trials[1] are work for an employer with a vacancy. They last for up to 15 working days, giving an employer the chance to try you out for a job before deciding whether to employ you. You remain on your benefit, or, if you are already on Welfare to Work activity where you are paid an allowance, you remain on that allowance.

Work Trials are available under a wide range of circumstances if you claim benefits or participate in welfare to work programmes. They will be organised by Jobcentre Plus advisers. They give you a chance to try out a job and the employer a chance to try you out. If you are a JSA claimant you should be aware that refusing a job, whether offered after a Work Trial or otherwise, can trigger benefit sanctions (see page 51).

The key benefits are:

• you can decide whether the job is suitable without losing your benefit: if you leave a Work Trial or decide you do not want the job your benefit is not affected

• you will be paid meals (up to £3 a day) and travel expenses (up to £10 a day)

• it gives you the opportunity to prove you can do the job

• it is a good way to persuade an employer to try you out

• it is an opportunity to find out what problems you may have in a working environment and get support to overcome them.

Work Trial vacancies

Jobcentre Plus should only let you go on a Work Trial where there is a genuine vacancy. Work Trials are normally full-time.

A Work Trial is voluntary and you can leave at any time.

Employer's contract

Before you begin your Work Trial, the employer must sign a contract with Jobcentre Plus:

- to give you the opportunity to do tasks which will provide suitable work preparation and experience
- to interview you as a potential permanent employee for the vacancy advertised, or another that they think you may be suitable for
- not to fill the vacancy you are on trial for until you have completed the Work Trial and have been interviewed
- to have Health and Safety arrangements in place.

Unauthorised absences and termination of the Work Trial

If you do not attend the Work Trial for more than 4 consecutive days, it will be assumed that you have withdrawn. Similarly, if you are sick and are likely to remain so for more than a few days, the Work Trial may be stopped. The employer can stop your Work Trial at any time because of changes in the operating needs of the organisation, or your behaviour or welfare.

The end of the Work Trial

If you are offered the job after the Work Trial and accept it, then the Work Trial has been successful. If you are not offered the job, your Jobcentre Plus personal adviser will provide an assessment of your performance during the Work Trial to work out why not.

Endnotes

[1] Jobcentre Plus Provider Guidance, Chapter 1, http://www.jobcentreplus.gov.uk/JCP/Partners/Providerguidance/index.html, accessed on 9 May 2007

Work Focused Interviews

What is a Work Focused Interview?

Work Focused Interviews (WFI) are designed to help people out of work to overcome their barriers to employment.[1] They require people making a new or repeat claim for certain benefits other than Jobseeker's Allowance to attend an interview with a Personal Adviser to talk through work options. People claiming Jobseeker's Allowance are required to attend a regular series of interviews and to provide evidence that they are taking steps to find employment. The requirements on people claiming the other benefits listed below are to discuss work options, where this is appropriate.

Warning: If you don't attend when required, your benefit may be affected

Note: If you attend an interview you do not have to accept work.

Work Focused Interviews (WFIs) aim to:

- encourage you to see work as a realistic option, where this is appropriate
- help you build upon your skills and potential
- help you tackle any obstacles to work
- offer you ongoing support through further interviews, or referral to other provision, for example New Deals.

Who is eligible for Work Focused Interviews?

To find out if you have to attend a WFI, answer the following questions:[2]

	YES	NO
Question 1 – Age Are you of working age (from 16 to 59)?	YES	NO
Question 2 – Work Are you not working, or working less than 16 hours a week on average?	YES	NO
Question 3 – Benefits Are you making a new or repeat claim for:[3] Income Support Incapacity Benefit Severe Disablement Allowance?	YES	NO
Question 4 - Where you live Do you live in a WFI area? A small number of areas have not yet received full Jobcentre Plus services, including WFIs.	YES	NO
If you answered **YES** to every question, then you probably do have to attend a WFI If you answered **NO** to any of the questions, then you do not have to attend a WFI		

If you have been claiming any of the benefits under Question 3 since before Work Focused Interviews were required, you will be required to attend 'Trigger point' interviews as discussed below (page 149) if you answered yes to the other questions.

Work Focused Interviews for Partners

You may also have to attend a WFI if you are the partner of someone claiming for certain benefits. To find out if you are a partner who must attend a Work Focused Interview for Partners answer the following questions:[4]

Question 1 – Benefits	YES	NO
Has your partner been receiving one of the benefits listed below and an increase for you, for at least 26 weeks:[5]		
Income Support		
Income-Based Jobseeker's Allowance (other than joint claim JSA)		
Incapacity Benefit		
Severe Disablement Allowance		
(To find out if you are eligible for these benefits see pages 14-15)		
Question 2 – Age Are you and your partner both aged under 60?	YES	NO
Question 3 – Work Are you working under 24 hours a week?	YES	NO
If you answered **YES** to every question, then you probably do have to attend an interview If you answered **NO** to any of the questions, then you will not have to go to the interview unless your circumstances change		

Who can choose to attend a WFI?

If you are claiming Carer's Allowance, Maternity Allowance or Industrial Injury Disablement Benefit, or you are aged between 60 and 65, you can choose to have a WFI voluntarily.

Arrangements, the interview and what to expect

Arranging the WFI

You will have a WFI before your first claim is processed if you are claiming Income Support.

If you are claiming Incapacity Benefit your initial meeting will take place eight weeks after the start of your claim.[6] The interview is mandatory (i.e. you must attend), although it can be deferred or waived by Jobcentre Plus (page 161).

Warning: If you fail to attend your benefit may be affected.

If you are eligible for a WFI because of the benefits your partner is claiming, Jobcentre Plus will contact you to arrange a WFI when your partner has been making the claim for around 26 weeks. The interview is mandatory (i.e. you must attend).

Warning: If you fail to attend without good cause your benefit may be affected.

If you are eligible for a WFI because of the benefits your partner is claiming, Jobcentre Plus will contact you to arrange a WFI when your partner has been making the claim for around 26 weeks. The interview is mandatory (i.e. you must attend).

Warning: If you fail to attend without good cause your partner's benefits may be affected. You should speak to someone at the Jobcentre Plus Contact Centre to arrange your interview or to let them know if you cannot attend.

Special cases

Special arrangements

In exceptional circumstances, for example owing to health problems or difficulties in arranging childcare, it may be possible for interviews to take place at home or away from the Jobcentre Plus office.

Translation

If you need someone to provide translation, this should be arranged for you. You can choose to bring a friend or a relative if you wish.

Arrangements should also be made if you are deaf or have a hearing impairment.

Assistance with costs

You may be eligible for assistance with travel and/or childcare costs if you:

* have a health condition or disability
* are a lone parent
* are a widow or widower
* are a carer

Overview of a Work Focused Interview

When you first attend you will have a meeting with a financial assessor that will take about twenty minutes. The financial assessor will first do an identity check and will then go over the details of your benefit claim. The Personal Adviser will then take over the meeting.

The interview with the Personal Adviser will last about 40 minutes. You will not be required to look for work, but the initial interview will tell you about the help you can get from Jobcentre Plus. The Adviser should try to take account of your individual situation when considering what advice to give you.

Participating

Participation means attending the WFI and answering certain questions about:[7]

- your educational qualifications
- your past employment history
- other work skills you have acquired or vocational training you have done
- whether you are currently doing any unpaid or paid work
- any medical conditions
- whether you have caring or childcare responsibilities
- your aspirations for future employment[8]
- vocational training you may wish to do
- your work-related abilities.

These questions are designed to establish basic information about you that will help the Personal Adviser to provide the right support for you.

Warning: If you do not answer the questions your benefit may be affected.

If you are a lone parent or are claiming Incapacity Benefit you will be required to help your Adviser to complete an Action Plan but you will not be required to comply with the content of the Action Plan.[9]

Trigger point interviews

Trigger point interviews are similar to the initial interview but will not include a discussion with a financial assessor.

Work Focused Interviews for Partners: if you are eligible, you will only have to attend a single WFI.

All other WFI interviews: if you are eligible, you will be invited for further interviews at certain trigger points. These interviews are mandatory.

Type of customer	2nd interview	3rd interview	4th interview	5th interview
Lone parent with youngest child aged 14 or over[10]	three months after first interview	three months later	three months later	three months later
Other lone parents	six months after first interview	six months later	12 months later	12 months later
Other customer	three years from date of last WFI or other face to face meeting with Personal Adviser	three years later	three years later	three years later

If you are a lone parent with a youngest child aged under 14, further interviews will be required at yearly intervals after the 5th interview.

Other trigger points

You can arrange further interviews at any point during your claim by contacting your Personal Adviser. However, there are other trigger points:

- when you start or end part-time work
- if you stay on Incapacity Benefit or Income Support following a Personal Capability Assessment
- when you reach the age of 18
- if your caring responsibilities finish or are reduced
- when you start or end a training course arranged by Jobcentre Plus.

Deferring or waiving interviews

In some circumstances the interview might be deferred (postponed) to a later date or you might not have to attend at all. You will be offered a deferral if it would be unreasonable for you to attend a WFI at this point, for example if you have just had a baby. Every situation will be considered on its own merits. If your interview is deferred you can still proceed with your benefit claim and start getting benefits as long as you agree to attend a WFI at a specified time in the future and actually do so[11] (although the date may be rearranged within limits).

The WFI will be waived when it is unlikely to be of any assistance to you in the foreseeable future, for example if you are very severely disabled. If your interview is waived you can proceed straight away with your benefit claim.

If you are 16 or 17

If you are 16 or 17 and are making a claim for a WFI benefit, you will have to attend a Learning Focused Interview (LFI). This will be held at a Careers Service or at Connexions. The interview will cover education, training and future work options. This is unlike the WFI in that you are not required to answer any particular questions. You may be entitled to help with travel costs.

Your first claim will be processed once you have attended the interview. However, you will not be required to attend any further interviews.

Sanctions

What happens if I do not attend?

If you fail to attend mandatory interviews, your benefit (or your partner's benefit[12]) may be reduced.[13] You will be given three chances to attend a WFI before any action is taken that could affect your benefit claim.

If you are late for an interview or make contact after the time of the interview has passed, you may be treated as having failed to attend. It is important to contact an Adviser as soon as you know you are unable to attend an appointment.

Where you have 'good cause' for not attending an interview, and show this to Jobcentre Plus within five working days after the date of the interview, you will not be regarded as having failed to attend. Otherwise, you may be regarded as having dropped your claim for benefit and will have to make a new claim and attend an interview.[14] Where it was not possible to show 'good cause' within five working days, the rules provide that you may be able to convince Jobcentre Plus both that you had 'good cause' and that it was impossible for you to notify Jobcentre Plus of the reason, without your benefit being affected. However, there is a time-limit of one month after the interview for this to be possible.

In all cases, where your claim is terminated (or not processed) because Jobcentre Plus has decided that you failed to attend an interview and had no 'good reason' for failing to attend, you have a right to appeal this decision[15] (see page 134 for details of the appeal procedure).

Acceptable reasons for non-attendance of interview ('good cause'):[16]

- if you can show that you did not understand that you had to attend an interview because of learning, language or literacy difficulties
- if you can show that you did not understand you had to attend an interview because your officer gave misleading information
- if you were attending a medical or dental appointment or accompanying someone you have to care for who had to attend such an appointment and it was not possible to rearrange the appointment
- if you had transport difficulties in getting to the interview
- if the customs and practices of your religion prevented you from attending at the time or on the day of the interview
- if you were attending an interview with a prospective employer
- if you were actively pursuing opportunities for work as a self-employed earner
- if someone who is dependent on you for care suffered an accident, a sudden illness or a relapse of a physical or mental health condition
- if you were attending a funeral for a close relative or close friend on the day of the interview
- if you suffer from a disability that made it impracticable for you to attend

Other factors may also be taken into account.

Endnotes

[1] Jobcentre Plus Decision Makers' Guide, Vol 1, Ch 5

[2] Reg 3, Social Security (Jobcentre Plus Interviews) Regulations 2002

[3] DWP, 'Changes to Work Focused Interviews' [December 2005] Touchbase 41, 23

[4] Reg 2(1,2), Social Security (Jobcentre Plus Interviews for Partners) Regulations 2003

[5] DMG, Vol 1, Ch 5, 05515

[6] DWP, 'Changes to Work Focused Interviews' [December 2005] Touchbase 41, 23

[7] Reg 11(2), Social Security (Jobcentre Plus Interviews) Regulations 2002

[8] DMG, Vol 1, Ch 5 (05032)

[9] DWP, 'Changes to Work Focused Interviews' [December 2005] Touchbase 41, 23

[10] DWP, 'Changes to Work Focused Interviews' [December 2005] Touchbase 41, 23

[11] DMG, Vol 1, Ch 5, 05039

[12] Reg 3(1), Social Security (Jobcentre Plus Interviews for Partners) Regulations 2003

[13] Reg 4(2), Social Security (Jobcentre Plus Interviews) Regulations 2002

[14] DMG, Vol 1, Ch 5, 05037, 05039

[15] DMG, Vol 1, Ch 5, 05090

[16] DMG, Vol 1, Ch 5, 05035

New Deal for Young People

What is New Deal for Young People?

The primary aim of the New Deal for Young People (NDYP)[1] is to move you into sustainable work. It provides a wide variety of support, including training, advice, jobsearch support and work experience.

NDYP consists of three stages:

- Gateway
- Four NDYP options
- Follow-through

Who is eligible for New Deal for Young People?

Compulsory or mandatory participation

If you are aged between 18 and your 25th birthday, and have been claiming Jobseeker's Allowance (see page 19 to find out if you are eligible for JSA) for six months, entry to NDYP is compulsory.[2]

Voluntary participation (early entry)

In some circumstances individuals are allowed early entry to NDYP. Personal Advisers use their discretion to determine which customers get early entry[3] but you may be eligible if you fall into one of the special groups below.[4] Around one in six starts to this New Deal are classed as early entry.[5] However, some in the special groups may be able to access other assistance through Progress2work (nationally) or Link-up (in specified areas). For further details see page 222.

Special groups:

- Refugees
- Ex-offenders
- Homeless people (including rough sleepers)
- People affected by drug addiction (including alcoholism)
- People who have been in residential care
- Ex-regular members of the armed forces
- Benefit recipients with language, literacy or numeracy problems
- Lone parents, people with disabilities and carers on JSA (instead of other benefits).

Gateway, Gateway to Work

Gateway

The Gateway period is the first stage of NDYP. It can last up to four months and may involve several different organisations. During this time you will remain on Jobseeker's Allowance and are subject to the normal Jobseeker's Allowance requirements of taking steps to look for work and being available to start work. The Gateway aims to prepare you for work by addressing any barriers, and to help you to find work.

Gateway content

The activity you undertake during the Gateway period will depend on your particular needs. Certain elements from the list below may be available to everyone, while other elements are only available to those with particular needs.

The Gateway can include:

- an initial phase of intensive help to find unsubsidised jobs, including help with searching for jobs
- independent careers advice, including motivation and confidence building and the identification of learning and training needs
- access to a mentor who will provide advice, guidance and encouragement on a non-official basis
- specialist assistance if you are disabled, from an ethnic minority, or have problems relating to homelessness, debt, drug or alcohol abuse[6]
- short refresher courses to help with basic and key skills, confidence and motivation
- referral onto Short Intensive Basic Skills provision (an eight week course)
- a Gateway to Work course to improve your chances of moving into work
- help preparing you to join a New Deal Option, including discussion with providers and taster options
- help if you are interested in self-employment including short awareness seminars, advice and information
- initial help with moving into self-employment which may include a basic awareness and information session, one-to-one counselling and a short four week part-time course at which you will develop a Business Plan.

The initial New Deal interview

The Gateway starts with an initial New Deal interview that is always undertaken by a Jobcentre Plus New Deal Personal Adviser. The interview will:

- tell you about New Deal, how it operates locally and the involvement of partner organizations
- begin the process of drawing up a New Deal Action Plan, that will record any action you plan to undertake and that you do undertake to move closer to work

- screen for basic skills needs
- where appropriate, refer you to partner organisations that deliver relevant activity

Subsequent interviews

Following the Initial New Deal Interview, you will attend interviews with your New Deal Personal Adviser on at least a weekly basis. These interviews will last around 30 minutes. Where you have significant barriers to employment due to health or disability that need addressing you should be referred to the Disability Employment Adviser, who will take on the role of New Deal Personal Adviser.

Gateway to Work courses

If you have not found work after four weeks on the Gateway you must attend a Gateway to Work course. The course is aimed to help you to improve:

- your communication skills
- how you present yourself
- your punctuality, time-keeping and time-management
- your team-working and problem-solving skills
- your ability to search for jobs, your CV, and your performance in interviews.

The course is mandatory and if you do not go your benefits may be affected. If no course is running then you must attend the next available one. The courses last two weeks, and you are required to attend for a minimum of 30 hours each week.

End of the Gateway

At the end of the Gateway period, if you have not found work, your New Deal Personal Adviser will work with you to find a suitable placement on one of the four options. You will also be referred to a Mentoring provider, although you will be able to opt out of this.

NDYP Options

New Deal for Young People Options

Once you enter the flexible options period you will be able to choose between four possible options. Your adviser will help you decide which is most appropriate for you. As well as your chosen Option, an equivalent of one day per week will be spent job searching.

At the end of week ten of your chosen Option you will need to go to a Jobcentre Plus office to discuss with your NDPA your progress towards the agreed objectives of your action plan and assess how ready you are to go into employment. Your adviser will decide whether you stay on your option for longer than 13 weeks and if so, by how long.[7]

1. Full-time Education or Training (FTET)

The FTET Option is designed to help jobseekers reach S/NVQ level 2 or equivalent, or offer support to those who have basic skills needs. The Option aims to equip those without a relevant S/NVQ level 2 or equivalent with the employability and occupational skills for work. Basic skills training is also available on this Option.

There are two types of programme:

- A short, job focused course that last eight weeks with a certificate awarded on completion
- A course of between 13 and 52 weeks with an education and training provider which will lead towards an S/NVQ level 2, involving work experience.[8]

2. Employment Option (EO)

The Employment Option offers a job with employed status with an employer, who is paid a subsidy of up to £60 a week to employ you.

You can participate in the Employment Option at any time during NDYP, including during the Gateway and Follow-through. The aim of the Employment Option is to help improve the participant's chances of finding permanent employment by offering a period of work with an element of training to an approved level. The length of this option is up to 26 weeks.

Employers will be expected to pay you the going rate for the job. They will be offered a subsidy towards the cost of employing you. If they take on a full-time employee (30 hours or more a week), they will receive up to £60 per week, and if they take on a part-time employee (24-29 hours a week) they will receive up to £40 per week.[9] They may also receive up to £750 towards the cost of certified vocational training.

The employer will sign an agreement stating that they will:

- keep you on as long as you show the aptitude and commitment needed
- provide or arrange training as appropriate
- monitor and record your progress and identify areas of action, in the same way as they would for any other employee to help them settle in and progress.

It is important that your personal adviser monitors your progress in the Employment Option. Details of the breakdown of hours must be specified on your Learning Development Plan and may be monitored by Jobcentre Plus.[10]

The Employment Option includes a Self-Employment Option that aims to prepare you to set up and run a successful business and to equip you with the transferable skills to help you into work with another employer if appropriate. It involves a basic awareness and information session, one-to-one counselling and a short part-time course that will include the development of a business plan. These elements of the Self-Employment provision are also available during the Gateway and Follow-through. During the Option period, the provision can also include test trading for up to 26 weeks and must also include some training.

Test trading enables you to start trading in your business while receiving a New Deal Allowance or benefits. Your profits are held in an account with the self-employment provider as joint signatory until you move into unsupported self-employment. You cannot use the profits to add to your income during this time, but can, by agreement, invest them in your business.[11]

3. Voluntary Sector Option (VSO)

This involves a work placement or employment in the voluntary sector to benefit your local community. It will also involve support and education or training towards an approved level. While this option can last up to six months, a decision will be made after ten weeks whether or not you need the full six months or whether three months is sufficient to enable you to re-enter the labour market.

4. Environment Task Force Option (ETFO)

This involves a work placement or employment in work designed to improve the environment, and will also include support and education or training towards an approved level.

If you participate in either the VSO or the ETFO, your participation will be reviewed at ten weeks and can then be extended to 13 weeks.

When taking part in any of the options you will need to ensure that your provider fills in an Action Plan Review Record and you obtain a copy for yourself. This records any changes to the Action plan and any progress you have made, ensuring that you are keeping in line with your goals.[12]

Finance and your choice of options

If you are on:

- the Employer Option: you will be paid a wage by the employer and will be eligible for tax credits and other in-work benefits (see page 238), but you will not be eligible for passported benefits such as free prescriptions or free dental care

- the Self-Employment Option: you will receive a training allowance from Jobcentre Plus which includes a top-up payment of £400 which will be paid to you by instalments. You may start trading whilst on this scheme.[13]

- the Full-time Education and Training Option: you will receive a training allowance equivalent to your Jobseeker's Allowance plus a training allowance of £15.38 per week, and travel expenses will be paid

- either the Environment Task Force or the Voluntary Sector Options: some providers will pay a wage, while others pay an allowance equivalent to your Jobseeker's Allowance plus £15.38 a week , plus travel expenses.[14]

Support while on a New Deal Option

While you are on a New Deal Option, you will still have access to your New Deal Personal Adviser and you should contact them if you have any problems. The adviser is supposed to keep in touch with you, and to monitor your progress throughout your time on your option.

Note: You are not required to attend weekly or fortnightly meetings.

The referral process

If you find it difficult to choose an option, you can do a taster that gives you the opportunity to try out one of the options for a short time. You can stay on JSA while doing a taster.

Once you have agreed to start an option you will have a pre-entry interview with your New Deal Personal Adviser. You will be asked to agree a personal development plan that will form part of the New Deal Action Plan.

Although you will have a choice about which option you join, once a decision is reached participation on the option is mandatory. If you repeatedly fail to start you may be sanctioned.

Transferring between Options

If one Option is not working for you, you may be able to move onto a different Option.[15] If you approach your Personal Adviser, they can agree to a transfer between providers and options.

Warning: If you simply leave and then try to claim Jobseeker's Allowance at a Jobcentre Plus office you will be referred for possible sanctions for leaving your option.

Where you are permitted to transfer from Full Time Education and Training Option, you can spend no more than 39 weeks on Options, i.e.

26 weeks on Full Time Education and Training Option, followed by 13 weeks on either Voluntary Sector or Environment Task Force Options, or a combination of both.

However, you can participate in the full 26 week Employment Option at any point during the Option period, even, for example, after a full 13 week Voluntary Sector or Environment Task Force Option, or after 52 weeks of Full Time Education and Training.

If you transfer within the same Option, you can only have a total of 26 weeks on the Employment Option (including the Self Employment route), 13 weeks, with extensions allowed in exceptional circumstances, on Voluntary Sector or Environment Task Force Options, and 52 weeks maximum on the Full Time Education and Training Option.

Follow-through

If you have completed your Option and remain without a job, you will have to re-claim Jobseeker's Allowance. At this point, you will be referred back to your New Deal Personal Adviser, who will start a Follow-through period.

You will receive intensive help to find jobs, as well as advice and guidance to identify further action to improve your prospects of finding work. You may be offered:

- jobsearch help including help with job applications, CVs and job interviews
- enhanced vacancy-filling services for employers
- work-trial placements with employers
- access to specialist programmes and measures where there are complex barriers to work because of disability.

Sanctions

Leaving the programme

If you are seriously considering giving up your option placement, you should discuss this with your Personal Adviser, who may be able to resolve the issue that is causing problems with your option, or may be able to refer you to an alternative placement.

You may leave New Deal to receive another benefit, for example, Income Support, Incapacity Benefit or Carers Allowance, if you fulfil the conditions for receipt of that benefit (to find out if you are eligible see page 64). Similarly, you can leave New Deal if you join a full-time education course or take up a job.

Note: New Deal for Young People is only available to Jobseeker's Allowance claimants, and if you cease to claim, other than because you have gone on an option or left to take up a job, then you automatically leave New Deal.

You can participate in the Employment Option at any time on NDYP including during Follow-through.

If you still require assistance to find employment, a further range of help is available through more intensive employment and training measures. The follow-through period can last for up to four months, during which time you will have interviews with your New Deal Personal Adviser. There is no set frequency for these meetings, and your adviser will agree a course of action that best suits you.

Warning: You can be sanctioned for repeatedly failing to start an Option, for leaving an Option without agreeing this with your Personal Adviser, or for being dismissed due to misconduct.[16] Jobcentre Plus is the only organisation that can sanction you.

A sanction could involve taking away two weeks' worth of benefit unless you have already been sanctioned in the last 12 months whilst on NDYP. This could rise to four weeks and after that up to 26 weeks if you have been previously sanctioned two or more times for an offence whilst on NDYP.[17]

Endnotes

[1] Jobcentre Plus Provider Guidance ch 11, and Jobcentre Plus Decision Makers' Guide, Vol 3, Ch 14

[2] Jobcentre Plus Provider Guidance, Ch 11, Para 2

[3] DWP 'New Deal streamlining changes' [June 2004] Touchbase 35, 20

[4] DWP. New Deal for Young People and Long-Term Unemployed People Aged 25+: Background Information. In DWP Resource Centre. Retrieved 28 February, 2006, from www.dwp.gov.uk/asd/ndyp.asp

[5] DWP. Retrieved 11 April 2007 from www.dwp.gov.uk/asd/asd1/tabtools/tabtool_nd.asp.

[6] DMG, Vol 3, Ch 14, 14111

[7] Jobcentre Plus Provider Guidance, Ch 11, Para 60

[8] Jobcentre Plus Provider Guidance, Ch 11, Para 1

[9] DWP. New Deal for employers. In Jobcentre Plus New Deal. Retrieved 28 February, 2006, from www.jobcentreplus.gov.uk/JCP/Employers/Ourservices/Programmes/New%5FDeal/

[10] Jobcentre Plus Provider Guidance, Ch 11, Para 19

[11] Jobcentre Plus Provider Guidance, Ch 11, Para 66 onwards

[12] Jobcentre Plus Provider Guidance, Ch 11, Para 66 onwards

[13] DMG, Vol 3, Ch 14, 14133

[14] DMG Vol 3, Ch14, 14143

[15] DWP 'New Deal streamlining changes' [June 2004] Touchbase 35, 20

[16] Jobcentre Plus Provider Guidance, Ch 11, Para 75 and 77, and Jobcentre Plus Decision Makers' Guide, Vol 3, Ch 14, 14225

[17] DMG Vol 3, Ch14, 14522

New Deal for 25 Plus

What is New Deal for 25 Plus?

New Deal for 25 Plus (ND25 Plus)[1] aims to help unemployed adults into sustained work. It provides a wide variety of individually tailored support, including training, advice, guidance and work experience.

ND25 Plus has three stages:

1. Gateway

2. Intensive Activity Period (IAP)

3. Follow-through

Who is eligible for New Deal for 25 Plus?

Compulsory participation

You are required to participate in the ND25 Plus if you:[2]

- are aged 25 or over
- have been claiming Jobseeker's Allowance for 18 out of the previous 21 months (even if you have just been receiving National Insurance Credits)
- do not live in an Employment Zone (EZ) area where there is alternative provision which you must participate in instead (to find out if you live in an EZ area see page 220).

Claimants for these purposes include both members of a Joint Claim couple if the claim satisfies the eligibility conditions.

If you are a Joint Claim couple the following matters are also taken into consideration:

- when a Joint Claim is considered to start
- when an existing Jobseeker's Allowance claimant claims for a new partner
- whether the claimant has any children who are no longer in full-time education or children who are over 18 years old

Voluntary participation (Early entry)

If you are claiming Pension Credit, you can voluntarily enter ND25 Plus.[3]

In some circumstances individuals are allowed early entry to ND25 Plus. Personal Advisers use their discretion to determine which customers enter early[4] but you may be eligible if you fall into one of the groups below.[5]

- ex-offenders
- refugees
- homeless people (including rough sleepers)
- people affected by drug addiction (including alcoholism)
- people who have been in residential care
- ex-regular members of armed forces
- benefit recipients with language, literacy or numeracy problems (if they do not enter Work Based Learning for Adults)
- lone parents, people with disabilities and carers on JSA (instead of other benefits).

Programme elements

The Gateway

The Gateway is the first stage in the ND25 Plus and lasts for up to four months. During this time you will have weekly meetings with and receive help from a New Deal Personal Adviser. You will remain on Jobseeker's Allowance and are subject to the normal Jobseeker's Allowance requirements of taking steps to look for work and being available to start work. The Gateway aims to help prepare you for work by addressing any barriers, and to help you to find unsubsidised employment. At least two of these interviews are mandatory and you will put your benefit at risk if you do not attend these. You will be informed which interviews are mandatory.[6]

Your Personal Adviser and their managers will review your progress at the end of the first and third months of the Gateway. They will agree suitable help that should be offered to you.[7]

Gateway content

The activity you undertake during the Gateway activity will depend on your particular needs. It can include:

- careers advice and guidance
- training needs analysis
- Basic Skills assessment and short Basic Skills courses
- short job-focused training courses covering key skills
- help with motivation and confidence building
- mentoring
- short work tasters
- short Intensive Activity Period (IAP) tasters
- initial help with moving into self-employment which may include a basic awareness and information session, and one-to-one counselling and a short four week part-time course at which you will develop a Business Plan
- support from a Music Industry Provider (MIP)

- specialist assistance to help improve job prospects and specialist help with other problems, such as homelessness, debt, alcohol, drug and substance misuse
- help for participants with a disability or health problem, jobseekers from ethnic minorities, or those in rural areas
- Gateway to Work courses which include training to improve communication skills, presentation, punctuality, time-keeping and time-management, and problem-solving and team-working.

At your initial interview you will begin the process of drawing up a New Deal Action Plan, which will record any action you plan to undertake and do undertake to move closer to work.

Intense activity period (IAP)

If you have not found work by the end of the Gateway, you will move into the Intensive Activity Period (IAP). This consists of flexible packages of support that can be tailored to suit your individual needs. Providers will record any action taken in your individual Action Plan.

The IAP is designed to:

- address 'deep-seated' barriers to work
- provide valuable experience of the world of work
- act as an added incentive to people to move into work

If you are between 25 and 49 years old, participation in the IAP is mandatory.[8]

Warning: If you do not take part, you risk losing your benefit.

If you are aged over 50 and are not claiming Pension Credit, you will be required to participate in the Gateway, but entry to the IAP will be voluntary.

For most people the IAP lasts for 13 weeks, however for those who need additional assistance it can last for up to 26 weeks. (In some circumstances this period can last up to 52 weeks.) About 11 weeks into the IAP there will be a review where the eventual length of the IAP will be finalised. In almost all cases you will be required to do a minimum of 30 hours of IAP activities, over five days.[9] If you have a health condition, disability or have caring responsibilities and have agreed restrictions as part of your Jobseeker's Agreement, you will be able to discuss with your NDPA about reducing these hours.[10] If you are working or studying part-time you are still required to take part in 30 hours a week of IAP activity. Your NDPA will work with you to arrange your study or work around any IAP activity and in certain circumstances they may be able to reduce the amount of time you have to spend on IAP activity to 20 hours. The study which you are doing must be helping towards getting a job.[11]

During IAP you will receive a training allowance that is equivalent to your Jobseeker's Allowance plus a top-up, currently £15.38, unless you are on some form of waged provision.[12]

IAP Routeway

In most cases the IAP is provided by a single organisation. This is called the IAP Routeway.

The IAP Routeway will:

- provide you with occupational skills such as motivation, timekeeping, communication
- support you in finding work which builds on those skills
- provide you with experience of a real work environment and a work reference
- encourage you to continue learning once in work

IAP content

Your IAP will consist of at least one of the following activities:

- help with basic skills problems
- work placements with employers (see also page 172). The employer is required to provide a reference.[13]
- work experience placements

- training with strong labour market links – short job-focused training or longer occupational training
- motivation, soft skills and job search skills provision
- any other support which will help you to overcome barriers to work
- help with moving into self-employment

Subsidised employment

You can move into subsidised employment from the fourth week of the Gateway, during the IAP and Follow-through. The job should be expected to last at least 26 weeks and wherever possible, be permanent. The subsidised employment element of the ND25 Plus differs from the New Deal for Young People in that there is no formal training commitment or payment for training accompanying the subsidy. However, employers will be expected to provide the participant with the same training as that undertaken by any of their other employees.

You will receive a wage, and employers will be expected to pay you the going rate for the job. They will be offered a subsidy towards the cost of employing you. Employers can receive £75 per week for six months if the post is full-time (30 hours or more), and £50 per week if the job is part-time (16 to 29 hours).[14]

Employers will sign an agreement stating that they will:

- keep you on as long as you show the aptitude and commitment they need
- give you the same preparation and training as anyone else doing the job
- monitor and record your progress and identify areas for action, as they would with any other employee to help them settle in and make progress

It may also be possible to do subsidised employment in conjunction with other Jobcentre Plus programmes such as Work Trials (see page 142).

IAP Training

Training is available to ND25 Plus participants as part of the IAP.

Education and Training Opportunities within the New Deal for 25 Plus

Education and Training Opportunities (ETO) are designed for those participants who face barriers to employment through their lack of educational qualifications following on from basic skills screening, assessment and subsequent training.

ETO provision can consist purely of Basic Skills provision (where it is for a relatively short period, for example an eight to ten week course) or can include Basic Skills provision as a minor element of a longer course.

ETO provision can last for up to 52 weeks. While on ETO you will work towards a recognised qualification, which can be up to NVQ level 3, or equivalent. ETO could include other elements, including help with IT skills, counselling to address personal problems, and financial advice.

ETO activities can be part-time with other IAP activities, such as work experience or work placements, making up full-time attendance.

Work experience within the IAP

The aim of work experience is to help you move into work, and where this is not possible, to improve your employability.

Work experience placements provide you with the opportunity to:

- develop or refresh soft skills and attributes
- update your CV
- gain a recent work reference
- undertake jobsearch which may include attending Jobcentre interviews

Work Experience Placements take place in a work environment with a provider but offer a higher level of support and supervision than you might expect at work. A work experience placement may be followed by a work placement with an employer, either within an overall period of work experience, or after a period of work experience. See also 'volunteering' on page 25.

Self-employment provision

The Self-employment provision aims to prepare you to set up and run a successful business and to equip you with the transferable skills to help you into work with another employer if appropriate. It involves a basic awareness and information session, one-to-one counselling and a short part-time course which will include the development of a business plan. These elements of the Self-employment provision are also available during the Gateway and Follow-through. During the IAP period, the provision can also include test-trading for up to 26 weeks.

Unlike what happens under the New Deal for Young People, training is not a compulsory element of the ND25 Plus Self-employment provision. It is available to you if you need some specific training in order for you to succeed during your test- trading but this does not necessarily have to be towards an approved qualification.

Follow-through support

If you reach the end of ND25 Plus and have been unsuccessful in gaining employment, you will return to JSA and move into Follow-through. Follow-through usually lasts six weeks but if you need additional help it may be extended to 13 weeks.

The support available will be tailored to your particular needs. It will include jobsearch support, guidance, training and specialist support, in addition to the help you received during the Gateway and IAP stages of ND25 Plus.

Leaving the programme

If you leave the New Deal programme without securing employment, you may be able to claim another benefit such as Incapacity Benefit, or you will have to re-claim Jobseeker's Allowance.

Warning: If you leave ND25 Plus without previously agreeing this with your New Deal Personal Adviser, of if you fail to turn up to appointments, you will be referred for possible sanctioning.[15] You will have to re-enter ND25 Plus and return to your NDPA who will decide which part of the scheme you should return to (i.e. the Gateway, IAP or Follow-through).[16]

Endnotes

1   See Jobcentre Plus Provider Guidance, and Jobcentre Plus Decision Makers' Guide for more information

2   Jobcentre Plus Decision Makers' Guide, Vol 3, Ch14, 14335

3   DWP 'Extra help for older people' [September 2004] Touchbase 36, 6

4   DWP 'New Deal streamlining changes' [June 2004] Touchbase 35, 20

5   DWP. New Deal for Young People and Long-Term Unemployed People Aged 25+: Background Information. In DWP Resource Centre. Retrieved 28 February, 2006, from www.dwp.gov.uk/asd/ndyp.asp

6   DMG, Vol 3, Ch 14. 1433

7   Jobcentre Provider Guidance, Ch 9, para 4

8   Jobcentre Plus Provider Guidance, Ch 9, para 8

9   DMG, Vol 3, Ch 14, 14342

10 Jobcentre Provider Guidance, Ch 9, para 9

11 Jobcentre Provider Guidance, Ch 9, para 10

12 DWP. New Deal 25 Plus. In Jobcentre Plus New Deal. Retrieved April 2007, from http://www.jobcentreplus.gov.uk/JCP/Customers/New_Deal/New_Deal_25_plus/index.html

13 Jobcentre Plus Provider Guidance, Ch 9, para 44

14 DWP. New Deal for employers. In Jobcentre Plus New Deal. Retrieved 28 February, 2006, from www.jobcentreplus.gov.uk/JCP/Employers/Ourservices/Programmes/New%5FDeal/

15 Reg 75(1)(a)(iv) Jobseeker's Allowance Regulations

16 Jobcentre Plus Provider Guidance, Ch 9, para 52

New Deal for 50 Plus

What is New Deal for 50 Plus?

New Deal for 50 Plus (ND50 Plus)[1] offers a route back into paid employment from being out of work for older workers. The New Deal for 50 Plus differs from New Deals for other groups in recognition of the difficulties that older people have in re-entering the labour market after becoming workless.

Note: The programme is entirely voluntary, which means that you will not lose any benefits if you decide not to take part.[2] You can take a job (including becoming self-employed) if you want to regardless of whether or not you will be better or worse off.

Who is eligible for New Deal for 50 Plus?

You are eligible[3] for ND50 Plus if you are aged 50 or over and have received one of the following benefits (to find out if you are eligible for these benefits see page 166) for at least 26 weeks:

- Income Support
- Jobseeker's Allowance
- Incapacity Benefit
- Severe Disablement Allowance
- Pension Credit

Note: Jobseeker's Allowance claimants aged 50 and over are also eligible for the New Deal for 25 Plus (see page 166) or Employment Zones (see page 214) which include mandatory elements.

You may also be eligible if you have been receiving National Insurance Credits or Carer's Allowance or Bereavement Allowance.

You are also eligible if your partner has been receiving one of the following benefits with an increase for you, for at least 26 weeks:

- Income Support
- Jobseeker's Allowance
- Severe Disablement Allowance

Programme elements

There are three elements to ND50 Plus:

1. Help to find paid employment through a New Deal personal adviser or to move into self-employment

2. Help in claiming the 50 Plus return to work element of the Working Tax Credit once you have secured paid employment

3. Access to a training grant once you have secured paid employment

You do not have to take part in all three elements of the programme, for example:

- The 50 Plus return to work element of the Working Tax Credit is independent of the New Deal for 50 Plus, so if you find work or become self-employed without using the New Deal, you can claim this element.
- You can find work or become self-employed without using the services of the job centre or the help of a personal adviser, and still claim your Training Grant.
- You can get help from a personal adviser to find work, but do not have to apply for the Training Grant.

Finding paid employment (caseloading)

Caseloading is a series of about six thirty-minute interviews with your personal adviser over a period of between three and six months. The amount of time will depend on your needs. Each interview will last 30 minutes. If you are disabled you may have interviews with a Disability Employment Adviser instead.

Note: During this caseloading period, your benefits will not be affected.

If you want to find paid employment with an employer, your personal adviser will help you by offering advice and assistance with writing CVs, writing application letters, and preparing for interviews, and will provide you with information about programmes and services that could help you. You will also receive money to cover the costs of travelling to interviews, including overnight stays.

Moving into self-employment

You could use ND50 Plus to start your own business and become self-employed.

You can participate in basic awareness and information sessions, one-to-one counselling and a short part-time course that will include the development of a business plan. You may also have the opportunity to do test-trading for up to 26 weeks, but this is not available to IB claimants.[4]

Additional elements

While on ND50 Plus, you may also have access to:

- Work Trials (see page 142)
- Travel to Interview scheme (see page 261)

Your New Deal Personal Adviser may also discuss with you the benefits of doing voluntary work, which you could do to develop and maintain new and existing skills, provide an up to date reference, open up job opportunities or provide you with a talking point at interviews.

The end of caseloading

Caseloading will end when:

- you move into a job or enter a training programme
- you no longer wish to participate (as the programme is voluntary)
- your Personal Adviser thinks this element is no longer appropriate
- you move into another New Deal or Employment Zone

Working Tax Credits and Training Grant

Working Tax Credits

ND50 Plus will give you help with access to Working Tax Credit payments:

- if you have found paid employment with an employer
- during your start-up year if you are self-employed.

ND50 Plus will give you help with access to Working Tax Credit: if you have found paid employment with an employer during your start-up year if you are self-employed.

Working Tax Credit is a payment from the Government designed to top up your wages that is paid through the tax credits system (see page 238). The 50 Plus element (if you are working less than 30 hours – £1,185, if you are working 30 hours or more – £1,770) is paid for one year if you are 50 or over and have just returned to work after being on benefits.

Training Grant

Once you have taken up work with the help of ND50 Plus and have successfully claimed the 50 Plus element of the Working Tax Credit, you can make a claim for a Training Grant up to the value of £1,500 where:

- £1,200 can be awarded at any time during the two year eligibility period for training that is relevant to your current job
- £300 can be awarded at any time during the two year eligibility period for lifelong learning.

The grant will be paid on production of a detailed receipt or invoice. It cannot be used to pay:

- for equipment (except workbooks or open learning)
- for job induction programmes
- for foreign language training unless this is a requirement of the job.

If you are self-employed, you could use the Training Grant to go on general courses such as business administration or marketing, which you would use to run and develop your business.

To start the process of claiming the Training Grant, you must complete an Individual Learning Plan, which you can get from the Jobcentre. Once the Individual Training Plan has been approved your personal adviser will help you complete the Training Grant Application Form.

Note: It is up to you to take advantage of the Training Grant. You have two years in which to claim it.

Leaving the programme

The programme is voluntary so you can leave at any time without your benefits being affected.

Endnotes

[1] DWP. New Deal for 50 Plus. In Jobcentre Plus New Deals. Retrieved 13 March 2007, from http://www.jobcentreplus.gov.uk/jcp/Customers/New_Deal/New_Deal_50_plus/ and Jobcentre Plus Provider Guidance, Ch 1, para 20

[2] Jobcentre Plus Provider Guidance, Ch 1, para 20

[3] DWP. New Deal for 50 Plus. In Jobcentre Plus New Deals. Retrieved 13 March 2007, from http://www.jobcentreplus.gov.uk/jcp/Customers/New_Deal/New_Deal_50_plus/

[4] 'Roadblock on the Route from Incapacity Benefit to Test-Trading'. In What's New?, retrieved 28 February, 2005.

New Deal for Lone Parents

What is New Deal for Lone Parents?

The New Deal for Lone Parents (NDLP)[1] (along with the New Deal for Partners, see page 196) is designed to help lone parents to improve their job readiness and increase their employment opportunities.

Who is eligible for New Deal for Lone Parents?

NDLP is a voluntary programme.[2]

You are eligible to participate in NDLP if you:[3]

- are aged 16 or over
- have a dependent child under 16
- are not working or are working less than 16 hours a week
- are not an asylum seeker

Note: If you are eligible but choose not to take part, your benefits or allowances will not be affected.

Programme elements

The programme elements are made up of a series of interviews between you and the New Deal Personal Adviser. The number and length of interviews will depend on you. Your adviser will give you help and advice about moving into work or training, as well as in work support to 'smooth' the transition into work.

Role of the New Deal Personal Adviser

Your Personal Adviser will offer a package of advice and support including:

- advice about job vacancies, jobsearch, writing applications and CVs, and interview technique
- calculation of how much better off you could be in a job
- explanation of the effect that starting work may have on your benefits or tax credits
- explanation of what benefits or tax credits you may be entitled to when you move into work
- providing access to specialist employment advice if you have a disability or health problem
- help for you to identify good quality registered childcare in your area
- help for you with expenses to attend meetings, job interviews or training which they arrange for you, including fares and registered childcare costs
- drawing up an Action Plan to monitor progress and record action
- arrangement of training to update skills and payment of the Training Premium, if you are eligible
- an in-work support service

Help with costs

When you attend an interview with a Personal Adviser or an employer you are eligible for help with the costs you incur. These include childcare and travel. You may also qualify for travel costs if you are attending approved training and other activities.

Training Premium

The Training Premium is a sum of £15, which is paid weekly in arrears, and is available to NDLP participants who undertake approved training for at least two hours a week.

Warning: If you receive a Training Premium it is your responsibility to tell the Inland Revenue that you are in receipt of NDLP funding and the Training Premium.

In most cases it would be anticipated that participants on NDLP and NDP who undertake training would attend at least 16 hours of training per week. These hours can be split between training and jobsearch according to your needs.

While on NDLP you will have access to a range of training provision. This includes:[4]

- training provision available via Work Based Learning for Adults (WBLA) and Training for Work (TfW) (except employed status WBLA and TfW) (see page 53)
- Work Trials and work experience (as part of an approved training course) (see page 142)
- NDYP Full Time Education and Training, Environmental Task Force, Voluntary Sector Options
- ND25 Plus IAP Education and Training
- ND25 Plus Self-employment Provision, including advice, training, the development of a business plan, and 26 week test-trading
- ND Music Industry Provider and Music Open Learning
- ND Basic Skills Training (non-Short Intensive Basic Skills)

- education and training available through the further education system, for which Income Support receipt provides eligibility for remission of fees.

Childcare

You can also receive funding for childcare provision while you attend approved activities or interviews, so long as the childcare is either:

- provided by carers registered with Ofsted (payment cannot be authorised for childcare provision by friends or family members unless they are registered childminders)
- run on school premises or by the Local Authority.

Childcare costs can be paid up to the first Tuesday in the September following your child's 15th birthday. The maximum amount of childcare costs payable depends on the amount of time you are spending attending approved activity or training, and on how many children you have.

Childcare Subsidy

The Childcare Subsidy is available to NDLP participants who move into part-time work of up to 16 hours. Help is available towards the cost of childcare while you are working, up to a maximum of £67.50 per week for one child and £100 per week for two or more children.[5] You are entitled to the Childcare Subsidy for a one-off period of 42 weeks. There is no help towards travel costs when undertaking part-time work.

The Childcare Assist scheme entitles all lone parents moving into work through the NDLP to funding to cover the costs of childcare for the first week of work.[6]

Additional support

If you are a healthcare professional, you could go on the NHS-funded return to practice course. This is specifically aimed at encouraging former healthcare professionals to return to the NHS. These courses are often funded by the NHS.[7]

If you live in certain areas, further support may be available:

- Lone Parent Work Search Premium (LPWSP), available in eight Districts, giving lone parents an extra £20 per week for jobsearch[8]
- Lone Parent In Work Credit (LPIWC), giving an extra £40 a week in work credit for up to 52 weeks, to all parents claiming certain benefits (London Districts), or lone parents claiming certain benefits (outside London).[9] The In Work Credit is piloting in a total of 22 areas. For London, the 2007 Budget announced that the Lone Parent In Work Credit was to be raised to £60 a week. PIWC is paid on top of tax credits.

Leaving the programmes

Since the programmes are voluntary you can leave at any time without your benefits being affected.

Additional programmes

New Deal Plus for Lone Parents

The New Deal Plus for Lone Parents adds an additional range of support to existing New Deal for Lone Parents provision. It is a pilot programme, available in seven Jobcentre Plus districts.

New Deal Plus for Lone Parents offers a comprehensive package of measures based around provision available nationally through NDLP, a core set of pilots and a range of additional measures that we believe will complement the NDLP and WFI models. All of this adds up to a single package offering:[10]

- a guarantee about a clear gain from work (In-Work Credit, tax credits), and some protection when work breaks down (In Work Emergencies Fund);
- a guarantee of support in finding appropriate childcare (brokered by Jobcentre Plus childcare partnership managers) and, in some cases, additional financial support for childcare; and
- a guarantee of the ongoing help of professional, well-trained and properly supported advisers (more adviser contact outside mandatory WFIs, more training, support and tools for lone parent personal advisers).

The New Deal Plus for Lone Parents adds a new, discretionary, In Work Emergency Fund that is available on top of the LPIWC available as part of the existing pilot programmes, and some more help with childcare. The DWP has now been convinced that keeping a job can be as significant as getting into a job, and that keeping jobs has been a problem for lone parents. The discretionary In Work Emergency Fund and the promise of better Adviser support for lone parents concerned that they might not be able to keep work up is a response to this issue.

The areas in which the New Deal Plus for Lone Parents is available are:

- Bradford
- Leicester
- Dudley and Sandwell
- North London
- South East London
- Edinburgh, Lothian and Borders
- Cardiff and Vale (Jobcentre Plus offices in the former Cardiff and Vale District within the South East Wales District)

It is proposed to extend this provision to all parents claiming benefits in London.

Endnotes

1 Jobcentre Plus Provider Guidance, Ch 13, and Decision Makers' Guide, Vol 3, Ch 14

2 Jobcentre Plus Decision Maker's Guide, Vol 3, Ch 14, 14402

3 DWP. New Deal for Lone Parents. In DWP Resource Centre. Retrieved 28 February, 2005, from www.dwp.gov.uk/asd/asd1/ndlp/NDLP_Background_Information.pdf

4 Jobcentre Plus Provider Guidance, Ch 13, para 1 and 14, and Jobcentre Plus Provider Guidance, Ch 14, paras 2 and 19

5 BBC. Paying for childcare. In BBC Parenting. Retrieved 28 February, from www.bbc.co.uk/parenting/childcare/paying_loneparents.shtml

6 HM Treasury, Child Poverty Review (Spending Review 2004), Ch 3

7 NHS. More information on www.nhscareers.nhs.uk/

8 DWP 'Disregard of Lone Parent Work Search Premium and Lone Parent In Work Credit' [2004] Housing Benefit and Council Tax Benefit Circular, HB/CTB A9

9 DWP 'Disregard of In Work Credit [2005] Housing Benefit and Council Tax Benefit Circular, HB/CTB G3

10 Description from 'Working for Children' DWP, March 2007.

16 New Deal for Disabled People

What is New Deal for Disabled People?

The New Deal for Disabled People (NDDP)[1] is a voluntary programme
designed to help people in receipt of a disability or health related benefit
to prepare for, find, and sustain paid work. NDDP Job Brokers will provide
help with looking for a job and any support or training that is needed.
It is also available as part of the menu of opportunities within areas
covered by the Pathways to Work pilots (see page 229).

Who is eligible for New Deal for Disabled People?

NDDP is a voluntary programme, so your benefits will not be affected if
you choose not to participate.

There is no qualifying length of incapacity. To participate in NDDP you
need to be between the age of 18 and pension age (60/65) and must
be in direct receipt of one or more of the following[2] (to find out if you are
eligible for these benefits see page 76):

- Incapacity Benefit
- a benefit equivalent to Incapacity Benefit that has been imported
  into the UK under the European Community Regulations on the co-
  ordination of social security and the terms of the European Economic
  Area Agreement
- National Insurance credits on the grounds of incapacity (which may
  be awarded on their own or in addition to payments of income related

benefits – Income Support, Housing Benefit, Council Tax Benefit, or War Pension)
- Income Support with a disability premium
- Income Support pending the result of an appeal against disallowance from Incapacity Benefit
- Severe Disablement Allowance
- Disability Living Allowance provided you are not in receipt of Jobseeker's Allowance, and you are not in paid work of 16 hours or more per week
- Housing Benefit with a disability premium, provided you are not in receipt of Jobseeker's Allowance, and you are not in paid work of 16 hours or more per week
- Council Tax Benefit with a disability premium, provided you are not in receipt of Jobseeker's Allowance, and you are not in paid work of 16 hours or more per week
- Industrial Injuries Disablement Benefit with an Unemployability Supplement

Note: If you are between 16 and 20 and registered with Connexions or the Careers Service and have a claim for one of the benefits above you are eligible for NDDP. In some other circumstances you may be entitled to participate if you are 16 or 17, or beyond state retirement age.

Programme elements

Once you have registered with a Job Broker you will have regular and direct contact with them regarding your search for work. The services they offer may include:

- offering careers advice
- assessing how taking a job would affect you financially, including information about in-work benefits
- offering basic training, for example on interview technique
- matching you to employers, by looking at your skills, interests and experience

- helping and advising on adaptations such as special chairs or computer equipment, and how to fund them
- an in-work support service for you and your employer to make sure the first few months in the job go smoothly.

Job Brokers have access to other Jobcentre Plus services and may refer you to another programme if you meet the eligibility criteria.

NDDP Job Brokers

Jobcentre Plus contracts a range of organisations to be Job Brokers. You need to register with a Job Broker to receive their services. It is up to you to choose a Job Broker. You can only register with one Broker at a time, and their services vary, so it is advisable to find out about all the different Brokers in your area and what services they offer before choosing one.

Jobcentre Plus Advisers can inform you about all the Job Brokers in your local area and the services they offer. This should happen at your initial Work-Focused Interview (see page 148) if you are making a claim for a disability or health related benefit. There is no formal referral to a Job Broker, but after the interview, you may be contacted to check whether you have registered with a Job Broker. If you have decided not to, the Adviser may offer you the opportunity for further interviews or referral to a Disability Employment Adviser.

You can find out which Job Brokers are in your area either by ringing the NDDP Helpline on 0800 137 177 (or textphone 0800 435 550), or by visiting www.jobbrokersearch.gov.uk

Note: If, once you have registered with a Job Broker, you feel you are not progressing, or you are unhappy with the service they are offering, you may de-register and then re-register with a different Job Broker.

Leaving the programme

There is no time limit for your participation on NDDP – you can continue to access support for as long as you want.

As NDDP is a voluntary programme you may choose to leave it at any time without it affecting your benefit. You are however encouraged to discuss any concerns with your Job Broker before you de-register.

Endnotes

1 DWP. 'New Deal for Disabled People'. In Jobcentre Plus New Deals. Retrieved 2 March 2005, from www.jobcentreplus.gov.uk/jcp/ Customers/New_Deal/New_Deal_for_Disabled_People/index.html

2 Directgov. 'New Deal for Disabled People'. In Directgov Disabled People. Retrieved 2 March 2005, from www.direct.gov.uk/ DisabledPeople/Employment/WorkSchemesAndProgrammes/ WorkSchemesArticles/fs/en?CONTENT_ID=4001963&chk=cV3TWD

New Deal for Partners

Who is eligible for New Deal for Partners?

You are eligible[1] if you are not working, or working less than 16 hours a week, and your partner is claiming one of the appropriate benefits listed below.[2]

You are counted as a partner if you are married or living together as if you were married, and your partner is claiming benefit for you[3] (to find out about eligibility for these benefits see pages 14-15).

Note: If your partner is on New Deal, Training for Work, or an Employment Zone, and you fulfil the other criteria, you are still eligible for NDP.

Note: You are not eligible if you have a Jobseeker's Allowance claim in your own right, or if you are making a Joint Claim for Jobseeker's Allowance.

Programme elements

The programme elements are made up of a series of interviews between you and the New Deal Personal Adviser. The number and length of interviews will depend on you. Your Adviser will give you help and advice about moving into work or training, as well as in-work support to 'smooth' the transition into work.

Role of the New Deal Personal Adviser

Your Personal Adviser will offer a package of advice and support including:

- advice about job vacancies, jobsearch, writing applications and CVs, and interview technique
- a calculation of how much better off you and your family might be if you start work. (N.B. it may be necessary for your partner to agree to their benefit details being used for this.)
- drawing up an Action Plan to monitor progress and record action
- advice about what benefits and incentives are available to help you when you start work, such as Childcare Subsidy and the Adviser Discretion Fund
- advice on childcare available locally (your adviser should have links to the local Sure Start for possible jobs, childcare help and so on)
- arrangement of training to update skills and payment of the Training Premium, if you are eligible
- an in-work support service

Help with costs

When you attend an interview with a Personal Adviser or an employer you are eligible for help with the costs you incur. These include childcare and travel. You may also qualify for travel costs if you are attending approved training and other activities.

Training Premium

The Training Premium is a sum of £15, which is paid weekly in arrears, and is available to NDP participants who undertake approved training for at least two hours a week.

Warning: If you receive a Training Premium it is your responsibility to tell the Inland Revenue that you are in receipt of NDP funding and the Training Premium.

In most cases it would be anticipated that participants on NDP would attend at least 16 hours of training per week. These hours can be split between training and jobsearch according to your needs.

While on NDP you will have access to a range of training provision. This includes:[4]

- training provision available via Training for Work in Scotland (TfW) (except employed status TfW) (see page 33)
- Work Trials and work experience (as part of an approved training course) (see page 142)
- NDYP Full Time Education and Training, Environmental Task Force, Voluntary Sector Options
- ND25 Plus IAP Education and Training
- ND25 Plus Self-employment Provision, including advice, training, the development of a business plan, and 26 week test-trading
- ND Music Industry Provider and Music Open Learning Provider
- ND Basic Skills Training (non-Short Intensive Basic Skills)
- education provision available through the further education system
- If waged provision is being considered, it should be made very clear that the partner or the primary benefit claimant may lose entitlement to passported benefits. It is however very unlikely that any NDP participants would choose this option in that event.[5]

Childcare

You can also receive funding for childcare provision while you attend approved activities or interviews, so long as the childcare is either:

- provided by carers registered with Ofsted (payment cannot be authorised for childcare provision by friends or family members unless they are registered childminders)
- run on school premises or by the Local Authority.

Childcare costs can be paid up to the first Tuesday in the September following your child's 15th birthday. The maximum amount of childcare costs payable depends on the amount of time you are spending attending approved activity or training, and on how many children you have.

Childcare Subsidy

The Childcare Subsidy is available to NDP participants who move into part-time work of up to 16 hours. Help is available towards the cost of childcare while you are working, up to a maximum of £67.50 per week for one child and £100 per week for two or more children.[6] You are entitled to the Childcare Subsidy for a one-off period of 42 weeks. There is no help towards travel costs when undertaking part-time work.

Additional support

If you are a healthcare professional, you could go on the NHS-funded return to practice course. This is specifically aimed at encouraging former healthcare professionals to return to the NHS. These courses are often funded by the NHS.[7]

If you live in certain areas, further support may be available:

- a Work Search Premium, available in eight Districts, giving those in a family in receipt of Working Tax Credit who agree to join NDP, an extra £20 per week for jobsearch for up to 26 weeks[8]
- In Work Credit (IWC), giving an extra £40 a week in work credit for up to 52 weeks, to all parents claiming certain benefits in London.[9] This is on top of Tax Credits.

Provisions NDP claimants are eligible for

Partner's Benefits

- Jobseeker's Allowance
- Income Support
- Incapacity Benefit
- Severe Disablement Allowance
- Carer's Allowance
- Pension Credit

You are also eligible if you are not working, or working less than 16 hours a week, and you or your partner are receiving Working Tax Credit.

Leaving the programmes

Since the programmes are voluntary you can leave at any time without your benefits being affected.

Endnotes

1   DWP, 'New Deal for Partners – new eligibility rules' [September 2004] Touchbase 36, 9

2   DMG, Vol 3, Chapter 14, 14401

3   Reg 2(1) Social Security (Jobcentre Plus Interviews for Partners) Regulation 2003

4   Jobcentre Plus Provider Guidance, ch 13, para 1 and 14, and Jobcentre Plus Provider Guidance, Ch 14, para 2 and 19

5   Jobcentre Provider Guidance, Ch 14, para 22

6   BBC. Paying for childcare. In BBC Parenting. Retrieved 28 February, from www.bbc.co.uk/parenting/childcare/paying_loneparents.shtml

7   NHS. More information on www.nhscareers.nhs.uk/

8   HM Treasury, Budget 2004, Ch 4,

9   DWP 'Disregard of In Work Credit [2005] Housing Benefit and Council Tax Benefit Circular, HB/CTB G3

18 New Deal for Skills

What is New Deal for Skills?

Vocational training for people claiming benefits is now primarily carried out by organisations in the educational sphere, rather than directly by Jobcentre Plus or by its contractors. The New Deal for Skills is a series of pilot schemes to ensure that people claiming benefits who have a lack of skills as their main barrier to work can be referred to learning providers and funded through vocational or basic skills training.

Post-16 education is devolved to national governments in Scotland and Wales, whereas Northern Ireland has a wholly distinct system. Therefore this discussion mainly covers the situation in England.

Who is eligible for New Deal for Skills?

All elements of the New Deal for Skills are available to people claiming Income Support or Incapacity Benefit as well as Jobseeker's Allowance if they meet certain criteria.

The New Deal for Skills is aimed at those 'for whom lack of skills is their main barrier to employment'. There have been difficulties identifying people who meet this objective, as many potential participants have been focused on other barriers to employment they may have, such as health problems for Incapacity Benefit claimants or family care duties for lone parents or carers. The New Deal for Skills follows from evidence that for disabled people, for example, those who claim Incapacity Benefit tend to have lower skill levels than people with similar health problems who are in work. Therefore, it is arguable whether it is the health problem or the lack of skills that is preventing the disabled person from working. Similar patterns apply to lone parents, with those who claim Income Support having lower qualifications than those with similar size and age families who are in work.

Programme elements

The New Deal for Skills comprises three elements, all of which are pilots only available in pilot areas. The pilots are entirely voluntary, and therefore carry no sanctions. The three elements can exist individually, or in combination in those areas where the pilots overlap.

The Adult Learning Option

The Adult Learning Option provides for longer term unemployed and inactive benefit[1] claimants to voluntarily take up full-time learning for up to 12 months, while inactive benefit claimants may continue to receive their benefits and in addition a £10 Training Allowance. Optionally, they may receive a Training Allowance from Jobcentre Plus equivalent to their benefit plus £10 having signed off their benefit. This is the only alternative for Jobseeeker's Allowance claimants.

As with other elements of the New Deal for Skills, referrals to the Adult Learning Option are only possible where the claimant both does not have a qualification equivalent to NVQ Level 2 and is assessed that the lack of such skills is the main barrier to entering work.

The learning possible under the Adult Learning Option is to enable those without a Level 2 equivalent qualification to gain a qualification at this level.

The Adult Learning Option is voluntary, but participation in the Option would be included within a Back to Work Plan, the preparation of which is mandatory in certain circumstances (see Income Support and Work Focused Interview chapters pages 64 and 144). Where Jobseeker's Allowance claimants are referred and agree to go onto the Adult Learning Option, then such participation is covered by the Jobseeker's Allowance regulations for programme participation (see Jobseeker's Allowance chapter page 18) that may incur sanctions for termination without good reason and for neglecting to avail of the opportunity.

There have been changes to benefit regulations[2] to ensure that Income Support and Incapacity Benefit claimants may continue to receive their benefits while in full-time learning. Participation for Jobseeker's Allowance customers is covered by earlier regulations.

The Adult Learning Option is available in five Jobcentre Plus Districts in England. These are:

- London Central and Lambeth
- Southwark and Wandsworth
- Greater Manchester
- Gloucestershire, Wiltshire and Swindon
- Birmingham and Solihull

Skills Coaching

Skills Coaching[3] provides information, advice and guidance assistance to the lowest qualified to access learning to improve their job prospects. However, the aim is for the Skills Coach to provide more intensive assistance than is provided by standard Information, Advice and Guidance services (advertised as the nextstep service[4]).

Skills Coaches are individuals who will develop a coaching relationship with you to enable you to identify your goals and aspirations, explore options and choices, and help you to make decisions about your learning path to skills development and sustainable employment. A unique feature of skills coaching is the in depth skills diagnostic. This will assess you against the skills requirements of the sector you are interested in entering. This leads on to the identification of skills needs and a learning path.

Skills Coaches will then help you to find learning opportunities and will remain in contact through the learning process to help you to move on into sustainable work afterwards.

Who is Skills Coaching for?

You may come into contact with a Skills Coach either by referral from

Jobcentre Plus or be contacted by the Skills Coaching service in your area (outreach). In both cases the Skills Coach will assess whether you are eligible. You must be 20 years of age or older to be eligible. You must also have the lack of skills as the main barrier to employment (and sustainable employment) and wish to address this need. Skills Coaches will need you to be committed to go through the Skills Coaching and learning processes if they are to commit time and effort to you.

In most areas, you must be a claimant of a Jobcentre Plus benefit to be eligible for assistance. While Jobseeker's Allowance claimants are eligible, the intention is for 80% of participants to be claimants of Incapacity Benefit or Income Support. Jobcentre Plus must agree that you enter the Skills Coaching process. There are a number of target groups, who must also be benefit claimants and meet the low skills as a barrier and commitment requirements. These are people aged 50 and over, black and minority ethnic groups and low skilled women.

In three areas an additional pilot includes those who are workless but not claiming benefit themselves. These are Leicestershire, Birmingham and Manchester.

Which areas is Skills Coaching available in?

- Birmingham and Solihull
- Cambridgeshire
- Derbyshire
- Devon
- Gloucestershire
- Greater Manchester (East, West and Central)
- Leicestershire
- London Central
- London East, West, North and South
- Nottinghamshire
- North Yorkshire
- Suffolk
- Surrey

- Sussex
- Tees Valley
- West Yorkshire
- Wiltshire & Swindon

These are defined as Learning and Skills Council areas rather than Jobcentre Plus Districts.

In a number of areas the Adult Learning Option is also available to you. The intention is to test whether the combination of the Adult Learning Option and Skills Coaching produces better results than Skills Coaching on its own (there is no area in which the Adult Learning Option is available without Skills Coaching also being available).

Skills Passport

The third element of the New Deal for Skills is the Skills Passport. This is intended to provide you with rather more than the elements of a CV by providing evidence of your progress and skill levels.

There are two different versions of the Skills Passport, a paper-based version and an online version that are being used as part of the Skills Coaching trials.

The Skills Passport provides you, and potential employers, with assurance that the skills you are claiming on your CV have been verified by independent bodies. The online version can contain scanned images of certificates that have been verified as genuine. Only the skills elements can be verified, and Skills Coaches may be able to verify possession of certificates and attendance on courses.

Endnotes

[1] Inactive benefits normally include Income Support, Incapacity Benefit, Carer's Allowance and Pension Credit (for those under state pension age).

[2] The Social Security (Adult Learning Option) Amendment Regulations 2006 (SI 2006 No. 2144)

[3] The Skills Coach Handbook, Learning and Skills Council, Coventry, 2006

[4] Website at www.nextstep.org.uk/

19 New Deal for Musicians

What is New Deal for Musicians?

New Deal for Musicians (NDfM)[1] is delivered to participants as part of New Deal for Young People and New Deal 25 Plus. It aims to help aspiring unemployed musicians into a sustainable career in the music industry either as artists under contract or as self-employed artists.

It does not directly provide musical tuition, but rather advice and guidance on the business aspects of work in the music industry. It caters for all genres of music including, rock/pop, dance, jazz, blues, country and folk, and classical. The provision is designed for musicians in a range of roles, including vocalists, composers, and performing DJs. It does not extend to those interested in careers allied to the music industry, such as management, technicians, and road crew.

NDfM can have three elements:

1. Access to advisory support from Specialist Music Industry Providers (MIP)

2. Full-time Education and Training Open Learning Pack from a Music Open Learning Provider (MOLP)

3. Subsidised or Self-Employment.

Who is eligible for New Deal for Musicians?

NDfM is available to jobseekers who are eligible for either New Deal for Young People (NDYP) or New Deal 25 Plus (ND25 Plus)[2] (to find out if you are eligible for these programmes see pages 154,166). It is a voluntary route within these programmes.

However, you will not automatically be allowed to participate in NDfM just because you are eligible for either of these New Deals and express an interest to do so. It will be left to the discretion of your Personal Adviser and an MIP to decide whether NDfM is suited to you. This will depend partly on whether you:

- are an active musician or have previously been working as an active musician
- have instrumental or other music-related qualifications
- have a work history within the music industry
- live where there is little or no local provision or would experience difficulty travelling to provision
- have a preferred learning style of independent study with access to support and would find regular timetabled attendance difficult because of your chosen career path

Programme elements

The scheme will last for a maximum of 13 weeks. An extension of an additional 13 weeks may be allowed in exceptional cases where a music industry professional can demonstrate to your NDPA that this is essential to your success of finding sustainable work.[3]

Your NDPA is responsible for supporting you through the scheme, including:

- identifying any barriers to participation you may face and discussing with you how you can overcome them
- informing you of the conditions for receiving your JSA or other allowances whilst on NDfM
- checking your attendance and progress during the scheme
- reviewing your goals and needs on completion of NDfM if it is necessary
- being responsible for determining any sanctions you may face if you have refused to accept reasonable offers of help in New Deal.[4]

Music Industry Provider (MIP)

You can request to be referred to an MIP at any time during New Deal. MIPs have extensive experience in the music industry and are able to provide impartial support and guidance, including advice about the business environment. They are not expected to assess your talent or abilities. The interviews with an MIP are in addition to the required hours on an Option or IAP. The use of an MIP is voluntary and is not a precondition for accessing support from a Music Open Learning Provider.

In association with your Personal Adviser, the MIP will help you draw up an Action Plan to monitor progress and record activities.

Your relationship with your MIP is confidential. MIPs are not required to disclose any information to your Personal Adviser without your consent. However, they are expected to provide information to enable your Personal Adviser to decide on the best way forward for you.

Meetings with MIPs can take place outside working hours and away from the Jobcentre Plus office or provider environment. Meetings with MIPs should be arranged between yourselves.

Your access to MIPs is intended to be flexible – you may see an MIP for your entire time on New Deal or just during the Gateway. MIPs will reimburse you with the travel costs of getting to interviews.

- Your MIP will be required to keep a NDfM activity log to record details of any activities you complete. It will also record your time-keeping abilities.
- You must write a letter to your MIP every two weeks to say that you are taking part in the scheme.
- If you fail to do this then your connection with your MIP will end.
- If you have caring responsibilities or health problems you must inform your NDPA and they may allow for your hours of activity to be reduced (to a minimum of 16 hours).[5]

Music Open Learning (MOL)

A set of specialist open learning materials can be accessed by anyone via the following website: www.ndfmlearning.com. They cover the subjects of the following available open learning modules:

- Music Industry and You
- Work and Jobs
- Creating
- Performing
- Recording and Production
- Marketing, Distribution, Promotion and Retails
- Copyright, Legal and Management
- Business and Money
- Teaching Music

NDYP participants

If you participate in NDfM within NDYP, you can access Music Open Learning through the Full Time Education and Training open learning route. The maximum time spent on this route will be 26 weeks. You will be required to complete an average of 30 hours' activity a week.

- You should be completing a minimum of 30 hours a week, although this may not be possible every week, for example when you may be performing or travelling.
- You must, however, complete a total of 390 hours of learning and associated activities, on the scheme.[6]

ND25 Plus participants

If you participate in NDfM within ND25 Plus, you can access up to 60 hours of music-related support during the Gateway and IAP, in addition to the 30 hours of required ND25 Plus activity per week. In exceptional circumstances it may be arranged for you to undertake more open learning activity, but this must still be in addition to your 30 hours of required activity.

Moving into Employment or Self-Employment

You can opt to move into subsidised employment at any time through NDYP and after the fourth week of the Gateway through ND25 Plus. Alternatively, you could try a Self-Employment route. You can access initial help during the Gateway. You will also have the opportunity to 'test-trade' (see page 159). This would normally happen during the Option/IAP period. Examples of test-trading include providing instrumental tuition, and performing at concerts or gigs. You could be part of a group or band of other musicians where one or more of the other members are employed. In these circumstances any earnings by the group will be apportioned and those relating to you will be held in a special dual-signature account with the self-employment provider until test-trading is completed. If you access NDfM through NDYP you can continue to use the open learning materials as part of the training element of Self-Employment.

Test-trading

- The time you are able to test-trade depends on how many weeks you have already spent on NDfM.

- The maximum time spent on NDfM is 26 weeks and so if you have already spent 13 weeks on this scheme, for example, you may only take part in test-trading for a further 13 weeks to make the total 26.

- If you do enter self-employment from NDfM then you are able to carry out any business; it does not need to be related to the music industry.[7]

For more information on Self-employment Provision available through ND25 Plus please see page 173. For more information on Self-employment Provision available through NDYP please see page 159.

Follow-through

Follow-through support and advice is available if you do not find work immediately at the end of your NDfM help.

Endnotes

1   Jobcentre Plus Provider Guidance, Ch 6, 134-190

2   Jobcentre Plus Provider Guidance, Ch 6, 134

3   Jobcentre Plus Provider guidance, Ch 5, Section 9

4   Jobcentre Plus Provider Guidance Ch 6, section 9

5   Jobcentre Plus Provider guidance, Ch 6, para 13

6   Jobcentre Plus Provider Guidance, Ch 6, Section 9

7   Jobcentre Plus Provider Guidance, Ch 6, section 9, Para 32

20 Employment Zones

What are Employment Zones?

Employment Zones (EZ)[1] aim to help long term unemployed people to move into sustainable employment. The thirteen zones operate in fifteen areas of the country which have high levels of long-term unemployment. Each Zone is designed slightly differently, depending on the contractor involved, but all operate within the same broad structure. Employment Zones operate by pooling funds for training, Jobcentre Plus support and the equivalent of benefit in order to maximise flexibility and give individuals more say in the choices which affect them. Participants are guaranteed an income equivalent to their net weekly benefit entitlement for as long as they remain unemployed.

The Department of Work and Pensions contracts service providers to run EZs. There are two types of contract – single provider Employment Zones where one contractor provides the service, and multiple provider Employment Zones where more than one contractor provides the service. Although the programme was initially introduced for long term unemployed people aged 25 or over, the Employment Zone approach now covers two further client groups: young people aged 18-24 years, who have already participated on New Deal for Young People, and lone parents. In areas with multiple providers, customer choice of provider is being introduced.

Who is eligible for Employment Zones?[2]

Compulsory participation

If you are aged between 25 and 60, you must take part in Employment Zones if:

- you live in an Employment Zone area
- you have been claiming Income-based Jobseeker's Allowance for 12 or 18 months (depending on the Zone).

If you are aged between 18 and 24, you must take part in Employment Zones if:

- you live in an Employment Zone area
- you have previously participated in New Deal for Young People
- you have been claiming Jobseeker's Allowance for at least six months without breaks totalling more than 28 days.

Note: You are not eligible if you have an outstanding referral to another programme, or are currently being sanctioned, disallowed or awaiting a decision outcome.

Warning: Once you have started on the Zone you cannot leave to join another Jobcentre Plus programme.

Voluntary participation

Lone parents who are claimants of Income Support may volunteer to take part in an Employment Zone in the same way as they may volunteer to take part in the New Deal for Lone Parents.

Early entry

In some circumstances individuals are allowed early entry to EZ. Jobcentre Plus Personal Advisers use their discretion to determine which customers enter early [3] but you may be eligible if you fall into one of the groups below.[4] As a newcomer you may be eligible.

Early entrant groups include:

- people with a physical or mental disability
- people who need help with reading, writing or numbers
- people whose first language is not English, Welsh or Gaelic

- anyone who is a lone parent who does not live with a partner and is responsible for at least one child living in their household
- people who have served in the regular armed forces
- people who were looked after as a child by a local authority
- people with a criminal record
- people with a drug problem
- people who have participated in Progress2work
- people who have been told by the Home Office that they are officially a refugee
- people who have been granted Discretionary Leave to Remain or Humanitarian Protection by an immigration office.

If you are an early entrant in a multiple provider EZ you will not be able to choose which contractor you go to. The contractor will be randomly selected for you. Once you start the EZ you must remain on the programme.

Lone parents

If you are a lone parent living in an EZ area you can volunteer for EZ help as long as:

- you are not working more than 16 hours a week
- you are not receiving Jobseeker's Allowance
- you are not an asylum seeker.

Note: You can choose to leave at any time and your benefits will not be affected.

In London, EZ provision has replaced the New Deal for Lone Parents. These Zones are delivered by multiple providers and you can choose which one you work with.

In EZ areas outside London, you can choose between New Deal for Lone Parents and any of the EZ providers in a multiple provider area, or New Deal for Lone Parents and the EZ provider in a single provider area.

Note: If you choose to participate in the EZ you can no longer participate in the New Deal for Lone Parents.

If you live in an Employment Zone area, and you are claiming Pension Credit[5] you may volunteer for Employment Zone help.

Warning: If you are a lone parent and fulfil the criteria for compulsory participation as a Jobseeker's Allowance claimant, you must take part in the EZ.

People claiming Pension Credit

If you are claiming Pension Credit and are not working more than 16 hours a week you can volunteer for EZ help.

Note: You can choose to leave at any time and your benefits will not be affected.

In the Multiple Provider EZs, people claiming Pension Credit can choose which of the contractors they wish to work with.

Programme elements

There are three stages within the Employment Zone. Each contractor has flexibility to design their own programme, while meeting the essential requirements outlined below.

Jobcentre Plus is responsible for identifying, referring and re-referring eligible jobseekers to the Employment Zone.

Customer choice model in multiple provider zones

If you are eligible to join the Programme you will have the opportunity to choose a Contractor operating the EZ Programme in the area in which you live. Once you have been directed to your chosen Contractor you will be required to complete the Programme with that Contractor.[6]

If you fail to choose a Contractor you will be randomly allocated to one of the Contractors in the Zone.

At the booking of the appropriate interview (18 months on JSA if you are aged 25 and over and six months on JSA if you are 18-24 years old and have previously participated in NDYP), you will be provided with the information leaflet. This will usually allow you a period of up to four weeks prior to the interview during which you can research the choice options available to you. You may have the opportunity to visit the EZ Contractors before making your choice.

Jobcentre Plus advisers will provide a signposting service where appropriate, whilst maintaining neutrality throughout the process.

Stage One

Stage One only applies to mandatory participants. Lone parent volunteers (and Pension Credit volunteers) will move straight to Stage Two.

Stage One lasts up to four weeks. You are appointed a Personal Adviser by the EZ contractor. They will help you draw up an individually tailored Action Plan. An Action Plan is an agreement between you and the EZ contractor. The Action Plan is an agreed plan of structured activities that will help you move closer to work. When this is agreed the EZ Contractor notifies Jobcentre Plus and you move to Stage Two, where the agreed activities are carried out. During Stage One you continue to attend the Jobcentre each fortnight and are paid IBJSA.

Stage Two

This stage can last up to 26 weeks. The contractor will enable you to carry out whatever activity was outlined in your individual Action Plan. You may receive financial assistance with travel and clothes for interviews. You may also receive training or assistance with moving into self-employment. You will also carry out an intensive jobsearch.

During this stage you will be paid your benefits by the provider and will no longer need to attend Jobcentre Plus.

Some participants will move directly from Stage 1 to Stage 3 without entering Stage 2 by finding a job.

Stage Three

Stage Three lasts 13 weeks and begins once you have started work. The contractor will provide in-work support to help you sustain work.

The EZ contractor receives a payment when you start work and a further payment if you are still in employment after thirteen weeks. As a result the contractor has a strong incentive to find you a job that lasts.

Follow-on

If you are a compulsory participant in an EZ and you have not found a job by the end of Stage 2 you will return to the Jobcentre Plus office to claim benefit. If you have been unsuccessful in obtaining a job after 26 weeks of active job-search in Stage 2 of the programme, you are re-mandated to Zones after a further 13 week period of claiming IBJSA.

Benefits and entitlements

If you are a voluntary participant your benefits will not be affected. If you are a compulsory participant, you will continue to receive your benefits or entitlements from Jobcentre Plus during Stage One, and during Stage Two you will receive from the contractor payments that are equivalent to benefit payments.

Leaving early

If you leave the EZ during Stage One and sign on within thirteen weeks, you will be referred back to the EZ immediately. If you leave during Stage One and don't sign on within thirteen weeks, you must re-qualify for the EZ.

If you leave during Stage Two or Three and your time on the EZ combined with your time in employment comes to less than 22 weeks, you will immediately be re-referred to the EZ contractor. If you leave during Stage Two or Three and your time on the EZ combined with your time in employment comes to more than 22 weeks, you must re-qualify for the EZ. If a participant enters Stage 3, but loses their job before they have been employed for 13 weeks, they return to the stage that they were on immediately before starting work and are able to continue with that stage until their total duration on that stage reaches the maximum number of weeks allowed on that stage.

Warning: If you are a compulsory participant, your benefits may be affected if you fail to do what is expected of you whilst on the EZ. Reasons for benefits sanctions might include:

• failing to turn up to appointments
• failing to comply with your Action Plan
• dismissal from an employment programme
• leaving early

Current Employment Zones[7]

The single provider Employment Zones are:

• Brighton and Hove
• Doncaster and Bassetlaw
• Heads of the Valleys, Caerphilly and Torfaen
• Middlesborough, Redcar and Cleveland
• North West Wales
• Nottingham
• Plymouth

The multiple provider Employment Zones are:

• Glasgow
• Liverpool and Sefton
• Birmingham
• Tower Hamlets and Newham
• Brent and Haringey
• Southwark.

Endnotes

1 DWP, 'Employment Zones: background information'. In DWP Resources. Retrieved, 3 March 2006, www.dwp.gov.uk/asd/emp_zones/EZ_Background_Information. pdf and DWP, 'Employment Zones'. Retrieved, 3 March 2006, from www. employmentzones.gov.uk/

2 DWP, 'Employment Zones – changes to the programme' [June 2004] Touchbase 35, 18

3 DWP. 'Employment Zones: background information'. In DWP Resources. Retrieved, 3 March 2006, www.dwp.gov.uk/asd/emp_zones/EZ_Background_Information. pdf

4 DWP. 'Employment Zones: background information'. In DWP Resources. Retrieved, 3 March 2006, www.dwp.gov.uk/asd/emp_zones/EZ_Background_Information. pdf

5 DWP, 'Extra help for older people' [September 2004] Touchbase 36, 6

6 Employment Zone guidance 20 Feb 2007, accessed 13 April 2007, from www.jobcentreplus.gov.uk/JCP/stellent/groups/jcp/documents/websitecontent/ dev_014072.pdf

7 DWP, 'Employment Zones'. Retrieved, 3 March 2006, from www.employmentzones.gov.uk/

21 LinkUP and Progress2work

What is Progress2work?

Progress2work[1] is a national programme aiming to support people with a history of drugs misuse to take up and remain engaged in mainstream provision, such as New Deal and Work-Based Learning for Adults, and to secure and sustain employment.

The programme has three key strands:

- contracted specialist providers of support, guidance and advice;
- awareness training for Jobcentre Plus staff so they are better able to identify and refer appropriate customers;
- a co-ordinator in every Jobcentre Plus District who links up key local partners and ensures that drug treatment and employment services are joined up effectively.

Who is eligible for Progress2work?

You are eligible[2] for the programme if you are disadvantaged in the labour market because of drug misuse, but have made sufficient progress in your recovery to be drug free or stabilised. This includes people who have completed a drug treatment programme, who are undergoing a drug treatment programme, or who are identified by Jobcentre Plus as recovering drug misusers.

In addition, you must be claiming one of the following benefits:

- Jobseeker's Allowance (see page 18)
- Income Support (see page 64)
- Incapacity Benefit (see page 76)
- Severe Disablement Allowance (see page 73)
- Disability Living Allowance (see page 116)
- Pension Credit (see pages 129-30)[3]

In exceptional cases you may be able to participate even if you are not claiming any benefits.

Note: Participation in Progress2work will not affect your benefits.

Programme elements

Specialist Employment Worker

If you participate in Progress2Work you will be allocated an employment support worker. They will work in consultation with other agencies with whom you are involved, such as Connexions. They will:

- assess your employment and drug-related history and any other factors that might impact on your chances of moving into and sustaining work
- work with you to draw up an individual action plan which will be updated to include planned and undertaken activities
- help you to prepare you for work, for example through providing confidence-building training and life skills
- help you to access specialist agencies to address any other issues that are acting as barriers to work, such as debt, housing, health and residual criminal justice issues.

The individual action plan will include not only the steps to move into work but also the additional activity that is required to supplement this activity. This will vary according to your specific needs and circumstances, but might include help to:

- access jobsearch training and resources;
- develop your 'soft skills'
- identify suitable work
- disclose your drug history
- access work tasters or work experience
- cope with any employer drug testing requirements
- disclose criminal convictions
- cope with the transition to employment and a wage
- manage transitional benefit issues.

Once you are ready to access the agreed employment measures, the employment worker will negotiate with the mainstream provider to make sure that the content and pace are suitable. The employment worker will continue to support you to complete the provision, and where the original plan is not working out, negotiate a revised programme.

Support will continue for up to 13 weeks after you have moved into work.

Leaving the programme

There is no fixed time for participation in the programme. Providers are expected to assess progress and take appropriate decisions about continuation. Progress2work is a voluntary programme so you can drop out at any time without your benefits being affected.

LinkUP

Jobcentre Plus has also introduced Progress2work-LinkUP. Progress2work-LinkUP provides employment-related support services for people facing significant labour market disadvantage due to an offending background, homelessness or alcohol misuse. It operates in a similar way to the Progress2work model.

It currently operates in the following areas:

- London South
- Liverpool
- Tayside
- Fife
- Bridgend Rhondda Cynon Taff
- Rotherham / Barnsley
- Bristol
- Bradford
- Manchester
- Lancashire West
- Berkshire
- Birmingham and Solihull
- Sheffield
- Greater Nottingham
- Gateshead and South Tyneside
- Eastern Valleys
- Glasgow
- Wakefield
- Lancashire East
- Knowsley and Sefton
- Leicester
- Sussex

Endnotes

1   DWP. 'Progress2work'. In Jobcentre Plus Progress2work. Retrieved 2 March 2006, from www.jobcentreplus.gov.uk/jcp/Partners/progress2work/index.html

2   DWP. 'Progress2work'. In Jobcentre Plus Progress2work. Retrieved 2 March 2006, from www.jobcentreplus.gov.uk/jcp/Partners/progress2work/index.html

3   DWP, 'Extra help for older people' [September 2004] Touchbase 36, 6

21

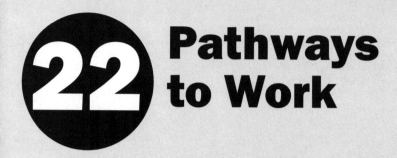

22 Pathways to Work

What is Pathways to Work?

The Pathways to Work areas[1] aim to help disabled people and people with health conditions claiming incapacity benefits to return to work. The pilots are officially regarded as successful and Pathways to Work is scheduled to be available nationally, but in areas not covered by the pilots in operation in 2007 will be provided by private or voluntary sector providers rather than by Jobcentre Plus.

Who is eligible for Pathways to Work?[2]

If you are making a new or repeat claim for Incapacity Benefit in one of the pilot areas you will automatically be screened for eligibility to participate in Pathways to Work. If you are making a new or repeat claim for Income Support on the grounds of incapacity, for Income Support whilst appealing against a decision that Incapacity Benefit is not payable, or for Severe Disablement Allowance at one of the Pathways to Work offices, you will also automatically be part of Pathways to Work.

If you are already receiving Incapacity Benefit or Income Support on health grounds you may be contacted to take part.

Note: If you are living in a pilot area and are receiving incapacity benefits you can volunteer to take part by contacting Jobcentre Plus.

Programme elements

Mandatory work-focused interviews

If you started an IB claim (excluding Personal Capability Assessment exempt cases) in the two years before the pilots started, you will have to take part in six mandatory work-focused interviews, unless the interview is waived because it is not appropriate or won't be of help. These are likely to be with the same adviser at monthly intervals. During the interviews the adviser will help you to identify future life and work goals and any barriers to achieving them, and will support you in overcoming these barriers. You will agree an Action Plan with your Adviser that outlines the activities that you will undertake. This will be reviewed at each meeting. Interviews can be postponed if appropriate.

Other elements

If you are a new or existing customer in a pilot area, you may be entitled to the following support:

- a job preparation premium of £20 per week for a maximum of 26 weeks if you agree an Action Plan and participate in activity that supports a return to work
- a Return to Work Credit of £40 per week if you move into work of 16 hours or more per week and earn less than £15,000 per year. This
- lasts for 52 weeks and is on top of tax credits
- access to existing training, employment programmes, and financial help, including the Adviser Discretion Fund (ADF) (see pages 249-50)
- access to the New Deal for Disabled People (see page 190)
- Condition Management Programmes – short courses run by local NHS providers that aim to help you to understand and manage your health condition.

Leaving the programme and sanctions

The only part of Pathways provision that is mandatory is the standard series of interviews with a Personal Adviser. The sanctions for non-attendance and the rules that apply are the same as those for Work-Focused Interviews (see pages 151-2).

You may leave the opportunities such as the Condition Management Programme or the New Deal for Disabled People at any time, as these elements are voluntary. If you cease to claim an eligible benefit you will also cease to be required to attend the mandatory work-focused interviews.

Current areas[3]

Jobcentre Plus delivers the Pathways service in the following 19 districts:

- Derbyshire
- Ayrshire, Dumfries, Galloway & Inverclyde
- Highland, Islands, Clyde Coast & Grampian
- South Wales Valleys
- Northumbria
- South Tyne & Wear Valley
- Essex
- Dorset & Somerset
- Lancashire
- Cumbria
- Glasgow
- Tees Valley
- South Yorkshire
- Lanarkshire and East Dunbartonshire
- Liverpool and Wirral
- Greater Manchester Central
- South West Wales
- Greater Mersey
- Staffordshire

Private and voluntary sector providers will start delivering the Pathways service to customers in fifteen Jobcentre Plus districts in October 2007. The fifteen districts are:

- Greater Manchester East & West
- Cardiff & Vale/South East Wales
- Forth Valley, Fife, Tayside
- North Wales & Powys
- Black Country
- City and East London
- Birmingham and Solihull
- Nottinghamshire
- West Yorkshire
- Edinburgh, Lothian & Borders
- Cornwall & Devon
- Central London
- Lincolnshire and Rutland
- Lambeth, Southwark and Wandsworth and
- Norfolk

Pathways to Work is set to be rolled out across the rest of the country by April 2008. It will continue to focus on new claimants, although existing claimants can voluntarily join the programme. Delivery will be through private and voluntary sector providers and new areas are:[4]

- North and North East London
- Cheshire & Warrington
- West of England
- Coventry & Warwickshire
- North/East Yorkshire and The Humber
- Brent Harrow & Hillingdon West London
- Marches
- Kent

- Leicester/Northants
- South and South East London
- Cambridge and Suffolk
- Gloucestershire Wiltshire & Swindon
- Surrey & Sussex
- Hampshire & Isle of Wight
- Bedfordshire & Hertfordshire
- Berks, Bucks & Oxfordshire.

Endnotes

[1] DWP, 'Pathways to Work'. In Jobcentre Plus Pathways to Work. Retrieved, 6 March 2006, from www.jobcentreplus.gov.uk/jcp/customers/programmesandservices/pathways_to_work/index.html

[2] DWP, 'Pathways to work' [September 2004] Touchbase 36, 17 and DWP, 'Pathways to Work' [June 2005] Touchbase 39, 10

[3] DWP, 'Pathways to Work'. In Jobcentre Plus Pathways to Work. Retrieved, 6 March 2006, from www.jobcentreplus.gov.uk/jcp/customers/programmesandservices/pathways_to_work/index.html and HM Treasury, Budget 2005, chapter 4

[4] Touchbase

23 Welfare to work pilots

Jobseeker Mandatory Activity

What is the Jobseeker Mandatory Activity Pilot?

The Jobseeker Mandatory Activity (JMA) Pilot[1] aims to help customers who are aged 25 or over to become better prepared for work, and to find work.

Who is eligible for the Jobseeker Mandatory Activity Pilot?

If you live in a pilot area, are aged 25 or over, and have been claiming Jobseeker's Allowance or National Insurance Credits on the grounds of unemployment for six months, you will be required to participate.

Warning: If you do not participate, your benefits may be affected.

Programme elements

The programme consists of:

- a three-day motivational course, that will be delivered by external providers, and will help you improve your job-search skills, explore your job goals, and draw up a Personal Action Plan;
- three mandatory follow-up interviews with a Personal Adviser who will help you to pursue your Action Plan and actively search for a job.

Leaving early

The programme is mandatory for those who fulfil the eligibility criteria, so if you leave early or fail to participate, your benefits are likely to be affected.

Pilot areas[2]

The JMA pilot started in April 2006 in:

- Bedfordshire and Hertfordshire
- Berkshire, Buckinghamshire and Oxfordshire
- Cheshire and Warrington
- Cumbria
- Lanarkshire and East Dunbartonshire
- South East Wales
- South London
- Staffordshire
- Surrey and Sussex
- West Yorkshire

Endnotes

[1]   DWP, 'Jobseeker Mandatory Activity' [March 2006] Touchbase 42, 7 and HM Treasury, Budget 2005, Ch 4

[2]   DWP, 'Jobseeker Mandatory Activity' [March 2006] Touchbase 42, 7

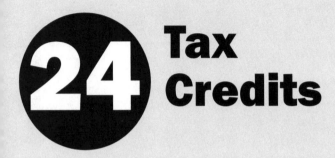

Tax Credits

There are two Tax Credits – Working Tax Credit and Child Tax Credit.

Working Tax Credit

What is Working Tax Credit ?

A regular payment made by Her Majesty's Revenue and Customs (HMRC) to people in paid work.

Who is entitled to Working Tax Credit ?

You can qualify for Working Tax Credit if:[1]

- you are aged 16 or over, you earn a low income, and either you or your partner is normally working for 16 hours or more per week and
- you have a dependent child or children or
- you have a physical or mental disability which puts you at a disadvantage in gaining employment. To qualify under this heading, you must:
    - currently receive a benefit for disability or incapacity for work or
    - you have received either Incapacity Benefit (long term rate or higher short term rate), Severe Disablement Allowance or a means-tested benefit disability premium at some time in the 182 days before your claim or a benefit for incapacity for work (including Income Support, occupational sick pay or Statutory Sick Pay) for at least 20 weeks within 56 days of making a Tax Credit claim or
    - you satisfy the rules for the 50-Plus element (this is paid for one year only) or

- you do not fit into one of the above categories but are aged 25 or over and normally working for a minimum of 30 hours a week.

Even if you are not in work, you should still be treated as if you are in full time work if:[2]

- you are not at work because of ordinary sick, maternity or paternity leave and receiving one of the statutory benefits for these
- you are on strike
- you were in full-time paid work within the last seven days
- you are employed, but you are suspended from work for disciplinary reasons.

Sometimes you may qualify for both WTC and Income Support or Income-based Jobseekers Allowance, for example, if you:

- receive WTC but you are off sick from your job
- are a term-time worker
- have a disability which reduces the pay or hours of work to 75% or less of people who are not disabled
- are a childminder.

In such cases, it is very important to obtain independent advice about which option is best for you.

Income and capital

When your eligibility for Working Tax Credit is assessed, annual income from the following sources will be taken into account:[3]

- gross earnings
- pensions
- profits from self-employment
- most social security benefits (but not Disability Living Allowance, Income Support, Housing Benefit, Council Tax Benefit, Child Benefit, Guardian's Allowance, Maternity Allowance, the lower rate of short-term Incapacity Benefit, Severe Disablement Allowance and benefits paid because of a work-related accident or disease).

If you are self-employed, your eligibility will be based on your profits in the most recent accounting period for which an Income Tax assessment has been made.

Income which is free of Income Tax is ignored.

All maintenance payments being received are ignored when working out Tax Credits. For lone parents, this provides a major incentive to maximise maintenance, particularly if they are in full-time paid work.

There is no capital cut-off for tax credits, and income from capital is treated like any other income. However, the first £300 a year of income from taxable savings and private/occupational pensions is disregarded and any income from tax-free savings will be ignored.

If you have earnings, these are some of the payments which are ignored:

- up to £100 a week of Statutory Maternity Pay
- Statutory Adoption and Statutory Paternity Pay
- Statutory Sick Pay
- reimbursed cost of expenses wholly, exclusively and necessarily incurred in your job (e.g. travel expenses)
- contributions made to an approved personal or occupational pension scheme.

How is Working Tax Credit calculated?[4]

The income threshold figure is £5,220 a year; if you earn less than this amount, you will be eligible for maximum Working Tax Credit. For every £1 you earn above the threshold figure, you will lose 37 pence off the maximum amount, until you are not entitled to anything.

Maximum Working Tax Credit is made up of the following elements (all figures are annual):

- Basic element (£1,730)
- Couple element (£1,700) – you are eligible for this if you have a partner, unless your only route to entitlement is by qualifying for the 50+ element and neither of you is working for at least 30 hours a week.

- Lone parent element (£1,700)

- Disability element (£2,310) – you are eligible for this if you or your partner have a physical or mental disability, which puts either of you at a disadvantage in getting a job (see below) and you also meet the disability benefit conditions (page 117). If you are a couple and this applies to both of you then you will get two disability elements.

- 30 hour element (£705) – you are eligible for this if you or your partner do paid work for at least 30 hours a week. If you or your partner are responsible for a child or young person then you are eligible for this element if your combined working time is at least 30 hours a week.

- Severe disability element (£980) – you are eligible for this if you get the higher rate of either Disability Living Allowance care component or Attendance Allowance (see page 117). If you have a partner and you are both severely disabled then you are eligible for two severe disability elements.

- 50 Plus element (if you are working less than 30 hours - £1,185; if you are working 30 hours or more - £1,770) – this is paid for one year if you are 50 or over and have just returned to work after being on benefits.

- Childcare element (80% of eligible childcare costs up to a maximum of £175 a week for one child or £300 a week for more than one child).

Disadvantage test for people who are disabled [5]

There are 21 criteria for this test, of which you must meet one. HMRC may ask you to nominate a professional involved in your care who can confirm how your mental or physical disability affects you, for example an occupational therapist, a nurse or doctor.

Examples of the criteria include:

- inability to balance unless supported

- registered blind or partially sighted in a register compiled by a local authority

- having difficulty with hearing

- a mental illness for which you receive regular treatment under the supervision of a medically qualified person.

Childcare cost eligibility[6]

Childcare costs must be for registered childcare for children under 15, or under 16 for disabled children (the definition of this is based on the disability element of the Child Tax Credit, see below). Eligible childcare includes care by:

- nurseries
- registered childminders
- certain approved childcare in the home
- other accredited providers and
- an out of hours or breakfast club run by a school or local authority.

You will need to be a lone parent to qualify, but couples can qualify if:

- you both work for at least 16 hours a week or
- one of you works at least 16 hours a week and the other is in receipt of one of the following disability benefits:
    - Short-term Incapacity Benefit at the higher rate
    - Long-term Incapacity Benefit
    - Attendance Allowance
    - Severe Disablement Allowance
    - Disability Living Allowance
    - Industrial Injuries Disablement Benefit with Constant Attendance Allowance.

Child Tax Credit

What is Child Tax Credit?

A benefit which is paid by HMRC to help with the costs of bringing up children.

Who is entitled to Child Tax Credit?[7]

You can receive Child Tax Credit if you have a dependent child or young person whom you are responsible for (which usually means they normally live with you) (see Chapter 24 for details), and you are aged 16 or over and are not subject to immigration restrictions.

To qualify, a child must be aged under 16 or aged between 16 and 20 and in full time 'non-advanced' education (i.e. up to the equivalent of A level or Scottish Higher or on an unwaged training scheme which is funded by the government). If they are aged 19, to qualify, they must have started their course or training before their 19th birthday.[8]

Your eligibility for the Child Tax Credit will be assessed at the same time as for Working Tax Credit. So you don't need to claim separately for each tax credit.

Income and Capital

This is assessed in the same way that income and capital are treated for Working Tax Credit (see page 239).

How is Child Tax Credit calculated?

The income threshold figure is £14,495; if your income is less than this amount, you will be eligible for maximum Child Tax Credit. For every £1 that your income is above the threshold figure, you will lose 37 pence, until the only amount remaining is the family element. All families with an income less than £50,000 can claim the full family element. For every £15.00 you earn above £50,000, you will lose £1, until you are not entitled to anything. This means that ninety percent of families are entitled to some Child Tax Credit.

Maximum Child Tax Credit is made up of the following elements (all figures are annual):[9]

- Family element (£545) – paid to all eligible families
- Family element baby addition (£545) – paid in addition to the family element for one year following a child's birth
- Child element (£1,845) – paid for each child within the family, including those under one year

- Disabled child element (£,2,440) – paid for each child within the family for whom Disability Living Allowance (DLA) is paid or who is registered blind
- severely disabled child element (£980) – paid for each child in the family for whom the higher rate care component of Disability Living Allowance is paid.

What happens if your circumstances change?

Tax Credits are calculated provisionally at the beginning of the claim with a final decision being made at the end of each tax year, when your entitlement and award is compared with your actual income. You are not obliged to tell HMRC if your income changes, but you risk an underpayment or overpayment at the end of the tax year if you do not do so.

There are some changes in circumstances which you have to inform HMRC about, for example if you change your employer, someone joins or leaves your family (e.g. you separate or have a new partner), if your hours of work vary around the 16 or 30 hour thresholds or if your childcare costs change by £10 or more a week for more than four weeks. There is a risk of a £300 penalty if you do not comply.

How do tax credits affect other benefits?

The amount of tax credit you are receiving is taken into account for Housing and Council Tax Benefits. If you are receiving Child Tax Credit, you are not eligible for child dependant additions within other benefits.

Any Child Tax Credit (and Child Benefit) you receive is ignored for Income Support or income-based Jobseeker's Allowance, but Working Tax Credit counts as income. The DWP and HMRC plan to move everyone with children who also receive Income Support or income-based Jobseeker's Allowance onto Child Tax Credit, possibly in 2008.

Overpayments

Overpayments of tax credits are common and many people have their tax credits reduced to pay back overpayments. This can cause difficulty. Overpayments usually come to light when HMRC look at the amount of tax credits awarded in the previous tax year and also when they are calculating your entitlement for the current tax year.

Overpayments may be caused by many things including errors by HMRC, or changes in your income or household which you did not tell HMRC about and they are very likely with a system which is based on annual income.

If your income increases HMRC will ignore an increase in income of up to £25,000.

HMRC must write and tell you if you have been overpaid and how much they will reduce your tax credits by in order for you to repay.[10]

If you receive Income Support or Income-based Jobseeker's Allowance your benefits do not increase to offset the reduced tax credits, but if you qualify for Housing and/or Council Tax Benefit without IS/IBJSA, these benefits are based on the tax credits you are actually paid after an overpayment is clawed back.

You can appeal against an overpayment if you think that the amount is wrong but you can't appeal against the HMRC decision that you must repay. However, the law gives HMRC a wide discretion to recover[11] and you can ask them to waive recovery. HMRC policy[12] is to waive recovery where:

- the overpayment was caused by HMRC error and when you were paid, you could not reasonably realise that you were being overpaid *or*
- recovery of the overpayment will cause you hardship.

They will also usually waive recovery of small overpayments up to £300.

Because there is a wide discretion, the above situations are not the only ones where legally, HMRC could waive recovery.

If repayment is causing you difficulty, you can reduce the amount you repay (which may be by making 'top-up payments' which effectively spreads the repayments over a longer period) and they will also suspend recovery action if you dispute the amount of the overpayment.

You can write and ask HMRC to waive recovery and if you do this, it is important to give full details of your circumstances, especially if you are asking them to waive on hardship grounds. But you may find that they refuse to waive recovery when you first ask. If this happens you can ask for your case to be considered by the HMRC Adjudicator or the Parliamentary Ombudsman (whom you contact via your local MP). In cases where HMRC have behaved unreasonably or very inflexibly, you may also be able to take a type of legal action known as judicial review.

Making work pay

Once you start work, several forms of financial assistance are in place to help ensure that you are better off in work than on benefits. These include:

- Working Tax Credit
- Child Tax Credit
- Job Grants
- Benefit Run-ons

In addition, if you are in work you may receive Housing Benefit, Council Tax Benefit (see Chapter 5) and In-Work Credits such as Lone Parent In-Work Credit (see Chapter 15) and Return to Work Credit (see Chapter 22).

Endnotes

1. Reg 4 Working Tax Credit (Entitlement and Maximum Rate) Regulations 2002

2. Regs 5 – 8 Working Tax Credit (Entitlement and Maximum Rate) Regulations 2002

3. Tax Credits (Definition and Calculation of Income) Regulations 2002

4. Tax Credits (Income Thresholds and Determination of Rates) Regulations 2002 & Tax Credits (Entitlement and Maximum Rate) Regulations 2002

5. Regs 9 – 9B & Sched 1 Working Tax Credit (Entitlement and Maximum Rate) Regulations 2002

6. Regs 13 – 16 Working Tax Credit (Entitlement and Maximum Rate) Regulations 2002

7. ss 3(3) and (7), 8 and 42 Tax Credits Act 2002 & regs 3-5 Child Tax Credit Regulations 2002

8. S8(4) Tax Credits Act 2002, & regs 2 and 5(1)-(3A) Child Tax Credit Regulations 2002

9. Regs 7 & 8 Child Tax Credit Regulations 2002

10. S28 Tax Credits Act 2002

11. Ss 28 & 29 Tax Credits Act 2002 – see use of words 'may' and 'recoverable'.

12. HMRC leaflet COP 26: What happens if we have paid you too much tax credit? Available on: www.hmrc.gov.uk

25 Payments for starting work

Job Grant

What is a Job Grant?

A £100 tax-free payment (£250 if you have a child/children) for people entering full-time paid work (16 or more hours a week or partner moving into 24 or more hours a week). It does not count as income or capital for means-tested benefits.

Who is entitled to a Job Grant?

You can claim a Job Grant if:

- you are aged 25 or over
- you have received Income Support, Jobseeker's Allowance, Incapacity Benefit, or Severe Disablement Allowance, or a combination of these for at least 26 weeks (if you have been on a New Deal or Employment Zone scheme, it counts towards the 26 weeks providing you were in receipt of Jobseeker's Allowance at the time) and
- the full-time work is expected to last five weeks or more.

If you are working part-time and the hours you are working increase to 16 or more, then you may also qualify for a Job Grant. Similarly, if your full-time work is self-employed, then you may be able to qualify.

A Job Grant should be paid automatically by Jobcentre Plus.

Please note that you are only able to receive one Job Grant during any 52 week period.

Adviser Discretion Fund

The Adviser Discretion Fund is held by Personal Advisers at Jobcentre Plus. From this fund, they can allocate up to £100 (more in exceptional circumstances and with the agreement of the Jobcentre Plus manager) to those on New Deal, and those who have been receiving the following benefits for 26 or more weeks:

- Jobseeker's Allowance
- Income Support
- Incapacity Benefit
- Carer's Allowance
- Severe Disablement Allowance
- Bereavement Allowance or
- Pension Credit

If your benefit has been sanctioned for even one day or your benefit stopped for at least one day in the last 26 weeks, you will not qualify until you have received the benefit for at least 26 weeks continuously.

The Adviser Discretion Fund is discretionary and there is no right to receive a payment. This is why the Fund is not publicised or advertised.[1] However, Jobcentre Plus staff should identify people who may benefit from use of the Fund.[2]

The Fund is designed to help overcome barriers to entering employment and can be made for items and services such as:

- initial childcare costs
- equipment, tools and work clothes
- initial travel costs

A payment cannot be made after someone has started work, and payments will also not be made:

- as an inducement by Jobcentre Plus staff for you to take up a job
- if funding is available elsewhere
- if you have capital or other funds you could use
- for everyday living costs
- to cover the costs of Criminal Record Bureau disclosure certificates (many employers ask you to obtain these)
- if you have had £100 in Adviser Discretion Fund payments within the last 12 months (unless the Jobcentre Plus manager agrees that there are exceptional circumstances)
- if you have not supplied receipts or proof of purchase for previous Fund payments
- if you have not repaid an overpayment of a previous Fund payment
- if there is evidence of fraud in a previous Fund application.

The Fund should be used where:

- it would make a significant difference to your chances of obtaining or accepting a job offer
- it would remove a barrier which prevents you from actively engaging in the labour market or accepting a job offer
- it would encourage you to take steps which you otherwise would not consider
- it is a sensible use of public funds.[3]

Adviser Discretion Fund payments are ignored as income for means-tested benefits, though they do count as capital (only an issue if you have nearly £6000 capital, in which case you would be expected to use this instead of having an Adviser Discretion Fund Payment).

If you are refused a payment there is no right of appeal to a Tribunal, but you can make a formal complaint to Jobcentre Plus and/or take the matter up with your MP.

Travel to Interview Scheme

The Travel to Interview Scheme (TIS) can help to pay the cost of travel and some other costs of job interviews.

The TIS will refund the costs of travel to a job interview and one or two unavoidable overnight stays. You will normally be paid the cost of public transport or the equivalent amount if you travel by car and you will receive a refund after the interview.

In order to qualify you must be receiving one of the following:

- Income Support
- Jobseeker's Allowance
- Incapacity Benefit
- Carer's Allowance
- Maternity Allowance
- Bereavement benefits
- a training allowance
- National Insurance credits (for example, because you are unemployed or incapable of work)

You must also meet the following conditions:

- You must have a definite job interview for a specific job which will be for at least 16 hours a week and which is expected to last for at least three months.
- You must have been living in your home area for at least four weeks.
- The interview is beyond 'normal daily travelling distance' (this varies from area to area and you will need to ask your local Jobcentre Plus office).
- You must apply before you go to the interview.

If the employer will reimburse your costs, you cannot get help and Jobcentre Plus will need to confirm with the employer that you have an interview and will also check that you attended.

More information: Jobcentre Plus leaflet Travel to Interview Scheme.

Endnotes

[1]   Jobcentre Plus internal guidance to staff on Adviser Discretion Fund. Retrieved March 2007.

[2]   Jobcentre Plus internal guidance to staff on Adviser Discretion Fund. Retrieved March 2007.

[3]   Jobcentre Plus internal guidance to staff on Adviser Discretion Fund section headed 'Essential Actions'. Retrieved March 2007.

Part 3: Making work pay - Payments for starting work

25

Benefit Run-ons

What are Benefit Run-ons?

Benefit Run-ons are periods where your benefit continues if you have been receiving benefits and have started paid work for at least 16 hours a week (or your partner does so for at least 24 hours a week). This helps to ease the transition from welfare to work.

There are three Benefit Run-ons:

- Mortgage Interest Run-on
- Extended Payment of Housing Benefit and
- Extended Payment of Council Tax Benefit.

Who is entitled to Benefit Run-ons?

You can claim a Benefit Run-on if you:[1]

- have been receiving Income Support or Income-based Jobseeker's Allowance or Incapacity Benefit or Severe Disablement Allowance for 26 weeks or more. This does not include any period of Mortgage Interest Run-on that you may have received in the past.
- notify your local Jobcentre Plus office (or local authority for Extended Payment of Housing/Council Tax Benefit) that you are working full-time (16 hours or more a week or partner is working for 24 or more hours a week), within four weeks of starting or increasing hours (this is a strict deadline), and
- have a job which is expected to last for five or more weeks.

If you have been receiving Jobseeker's Allowance, it is important not to just stop signing on if you get a job, but to inform Jobcentre Plus that you have started work so that any appropriate run-on is then paid.

Mortgage Interest Run-on

This allows you to continue receiving Income Support or Income-based Jobseeker's Allowance to cover some of your mortgage or housing loan interest for up to four weeks after you start full-time work.

Housing Benefit Extended Payment

This allows you to continue receive maximum Housing Benefit for up to four weeks after you have started full-time work, at the same rate as when you were on Income Support, Income-based Jobseeker's Allowance, Incapacity Benefit or Severe Disablement Allowance.

After the four-week period, you may be able to continue receiving some Housing Benefit if you are in full-time work. This will depend on:

- the level of rent you are paying
- your income
- your savings and capital, and
- your personal or family circumstances.

If you claim Housing Benefit or Council Tax Benefit, having previously received Extended Housing Benefit or Extended Council Tax Benefit, then your claim should be fast-tracked and dealt with within seven days of making a new claim.

Extended Council Tax Benefit

The rules for Extended Council Tax Benefit are the same as for Extended Housing Benefit.

For more details about Housing and Council Tax Benefits, see page 90.

Endnotes

[1] Reg 72 & Sch 7 Housing Benefit Regulations 2006 & Reg 60 & Sch 6 Council Tax Benefit Regulations 2006

Useful contacts

Useful books about benefit rights

Welfare Benefits & Tax Credits Handbook 2007/08 (Child Poverty Action Group)

Lone Parent Handbook 2006/07 (One Parent Families)

Disability Rights Handbook 2007-2008 (Disability Alliance)

Jobs

Department for Work and Pensions

The Department for Work and Pensions can be contacted at www.dwp.gov.uk

Directgov: Employment

This website offers help and advice for anyone who is in work or looking for work and training.

www.direct.gov.uk/en/Employment

Jobcentre Plus

The Jobcentre Plus website is www.jobcentreplus.gov.uk. Details of all local Jobcentre Plus offices can be found here. The website also lists who you need to contact if you have a complaint, query or suggestion.

If you are a jobseeker, you can call Jobseeker Direct: 0845 6060 234

Children and Young People

Connexions

The Connexions Service was set up to give all 13-19 year olds in England a better start in life, providing integrated information, advice and guidance. Visit the Connexions website: www.connexions-direct.com/. Alternatively, you can contact an adviser by calling: 080 800 13 2 19.

Child Poverty Action Group (CPAG)

CPAG promotes action for the relief, directly or indirectly, of poverty among children and families with children. It works to ensure that those on low incomes get their full entitlement to welfare benefits. It published several books detailing the current information on welfare rights and social policy issues. Contact details:

94 White Lion Street, London N1 9PF
Tel: 020 7837 7979   Fax: 020 7837 6414
Email: staff@cpag.org.uk
Website: http://www.cpag.org.uk/

CPAG in Scotland

Unit 09 Ladywell
94 Duke Street
Glasgow G4 0UW
General queries: 0141 5552 3303

Advice line

(Advice agencies in Scotland only, Tuesday and Wednesday 10am-12 noon)

Tel: 0141 552 0552   Fax: 0141 552 4404
Email: staff@cpagscotland.org.uk
Website: www.cpag.org.uk/

Child Support Agency

The Child Support Agency exists to ensure that, where an application for child maintenance has been made, parents who live apart contribute financially to the upkeep of their children. You can find out more by visiting their website: www.csa.gov.uk/. You can also contact their national helpline: 08457 133 133

The Prince's Trust

The Prince's Trust offers a range of services to young people (aged 18-30) including educational underachievers, refugees and asylum seekers, unemployed, in/leaving care.

Website: www.princes-trust.org.uk
Email: info@princes-trust.org.uk
Telephone: 0800 842 842

Lone Parents

Gingerbread

Gingerbread supports one parent families via local contact groups and a helpline: 0800 018 4318 or online at www.gingerbread.org.uk.

National Helpline

There is a New Deal for Lone Parents freephone helpline number: 0800 868 868

One Parent Families

This charity provides help and advice to lone parent families. You can call their advice line: 0800 018 5026, Monday to Friday 9am to 5pm, Wednesdays 9am to 8pm. Or, visit their website for more information: www.oneparentfamilies.org.uk

Equality

Commission for Racial Equality (CRE)

The CRE is a publicly funded, non-governmental body set up under the

Race Relations Act 1976 to tackle racial discrimination and promote racial equality. Contact the CRE at:

St Dunstan's House
201-211 Borough High Street, London SE1 1GZ
Tel: 020 7939 0000   Fax: 020 7939 0001
Email: info@cre.gov.uk
Website: www.cre.gov.uk

Equal Opportunities Commission

The EOC was set up as an independent statutory body with the following powers:

- to work towards the elimination of discrimination on the grounds of sex or marriage
- to promote equality of opportunity for women and men
- to keep under review the Sex Discrimination Act and the Equal Pay Act.

It provides up-to-date advice on your rights and produces straightforward information to help individuals and employers. It offers a helpline to the public. Call 08456 015901. Visit the website at www.eoc.org.uk.

Disability Rights Commission (DRC)

The DRC is an independent body set up by the Government to help secure civil rights for disabled people. It offers a helpline for the public which is open 8.00am to 8.00pm Monday to Friday:

Tel: 08457 622 633   Fax: 08457 778 878
Textphone: 08457 622 644

DRC Helpline

Freepost MID 02164, Stratford-upon-Avon CV37 9HY
Email: enquiry@drc-gb.org
Website: www.drc-gb.org

The DRC helpline provides information and advice about all aspects of the Disability Discrimination Act, as well is can offer good practice advice on the employment of disabled people.

Age Concern

Age concern provides an information line that offers detailed information to older people and their families on a range of issues and benefits, care and housing. It is open 7 days a week from 8am-7pm. Visit their website: www.ageconcern.org.uk or call the free helpline: 0800 00 99 66.

Employment Relations

ACAS

ACAS is the employment relations expert. It can offer free impartial help and information to people experiencing problems with employment issues on its helpline service at 0845 747 747. Visit the ACAS website: www.acas.org.uk/.

ACAS has an office base in seven regions of England. The head office address is:

Brandon House. 180 Borough High Street, London SE1 1LW

Health and Safety Executive (HSE)

The HSE ensures that risks to people's health and safety from work activities are properly controlled. It offers an information line to the public: 0845 345 0055.You can also visit their website for more information: www.hse.gov.uk.

Trades Union Congress

The TUC is the voice of Britain at work. With 71 affiliated unions representing nearly seven million working people from all walks of life, they campaign for a fair deal at work and for social justice at home and abroad.

The TUC is based at:
Congress House, Great Russell Street, London WC1B 3LS
Tel: 020 7636 4030
Website: www.tuc.org.uk

Training

Department for Education and Skills (DfES)

The DfES aims to give children an excellent start in education, enable young people to equip themselves with life and work skills, and encourage adults to achieve their full potential through learning.

Contact the Department via email at info@dfes.gsi.gov.uk or by telephone on 0870 000 2288. The website is at www.dfes.gov.uk.

Learning and Skills Council (LSC)

The LSC is responsible for funding and planning education and training for over 16-year-olds in England.

For general enquiries, contact the LSC helpline on 0870 900 6800 or email info@lsc.gov.uk. If you have a query about provision in your area, there is a comprehensive email list of the 49 local LSCs on the main website at www.lsc.gov.uk.

Other

Citizens Advice Bureau

The Citizens Advice Bureau (CAB) provide advice on a range of issues. A directory of local telephone numbers is on their website at www.citizensadvice.org.uk.

Refugee Council

If you are a migrant, seek advice from a professional. Initial help for asylum seekers, those with Exceptional Leave to Remain or Humanitarian Protection and refugees can be found at the Refugee Council on 020 7346 6700or online at www.refugeecouncil.org.uk.

Shelter

If you need housing advice, particularly if you are without a home, Shelter offers a freephone number, 0808 800 444, or visit them online at www.shelter.org.uk.

28 PCA indicators

Personal Capability Assessment (PCA) Descriptors[1]

To be treated as incapable of work, you must score a total of either:[2]

- 15 points from the physical abilities list; or
- ten points from the mental abilities list; or
- 15 points if you have a combination of physical and mental incapacity.

If you have a combination of mental and physical disabilities and you score between six and nine (inclusive) in the mental disability list, then a score of nine is added to the physical test. Scores of less than six are ignored.

To assess your score:

For physical disabilities, start at the bottom of each activity and stop when you get to the highest descriptor and score. This will be your score, if any, for that activity. If you can score under both physical activities 1 & 2 (walking on level ground and up/down stairs) you can only count whichever score is the highest, not scores from both activities.

For mental disabilities, you may collect more than one score for each activity.[3]

Part 1 – Physical disabilities

Activity	Descriptor	Points
(1) Walking on level ground with a walking stick or other aid if such aid is normally used.	**(a) Cannot walk at all.**	15
	(b) Cannot walk more than a few steps without stopping or severe discomfort.	15
	(c) Cannot walk more than 50 metres without stopping or severe discomfort.	15
	(d) Cannot walk more than 200 metres without stopping or severe discomfort.	7
	(e) Cannot walk more than 400 metres without stopping or severe discomfort.	3
	(f) Cannot walk more than 800 metres without stopping or severe discomfort.	0
	(g) No walking problem.	0
(2) Walking up and down stairs.	**(a) Cannot walk up and down one stair.**	15
	(b) Cannot walk up and down a flight of 12 stairs	15
	(c) Cannot walk up and down a flight of 12 stairs without holding on and taking rest.	7
	(d) Cannot walk up and down a flight of 12 stairs without holding on.	3
	(e) Can only walk up and down a flight of 12 stairs if he goes sideways or one step at a time.	3
	(f) No problem in walking up and down stairs.	0

Part 1 – Physical disabilities (continued)

Activity	Descriptor	Points
(3) Sitting in an upright chair with a back, but no arms.	a) Cannot sit comfortably	15
	b) Cannot sit comfortably for more than ten minutes without having to move from the chair because the degree of discomfort makes it impossible to continue sitting.	15
	(c) Cannot sit comfortably for more than 30 minutes without having to move from the chair because the degree of discomfort makes it impossible to continue sitting.	7
	(d) Cannot sit comfortably for more than one hour without having to move from the chair because the degree of discomfort makes it impossible to continue sitting.	3
	(e) Cannot sit comfortably for more than two hours without having to move from the chair because the degree of discomfort makes it impossible to continue sitting.	0
	(f) No problem with sitting.	0
(4) Standing without the support of another person or the use of an aid except a walking stick	(a) Cannot stand unassisted.	15
	(b) Cannot stand for more than a minute before needing to sit down.	15
	(c) Cannot stand for more than ten minutes before needing to sit down.	15
	(d) Cannot stand for more than 30 minutes before needing to sit down.	7
	(e) Cannot stand for more than ten minutes before needing to move around.	7
	(f) Cannot stand for more than 30 minutes before needing to move around.	3
	(g) No problem standing.	0

Part 1 – Physical disabilities (continued)

Activity	Descriptor	Points
(5) Rising from sitting in an upright chair with a back but no arms without the help of another person.	**(a) Cannot rise from sitting to standing.**	15
	(b) Cannot rise from sitting to standing without holding on to something.	7
	(c) Sometimes cannot rise from sitting to standing without holding onto something.	3
	(d) No problem with rising from sitting to standing.	0
(6) Bending and kneeling	**(a) Cannot bend to touch his knees and straighten up again.**	15
	(b) Cannot either bend or kneel, or bend and kneel as if to pick up a piece of paper from the floor and straighten up again.	15
	(c) Sometimes cannot either bend or kneel, or bend and kneel as if to pick up a piece of paper from the floor and straighten up again.	3
	(d) No problem with bending and kneeling.	0
(7) Manual dexterity	**(a) Cannot turn the pages of a book with either hand.**	15
	(b) Cannot turn a sink tap or the control knobs on a cooker with either hand.	15
	(c) Cannot pick up a coin which is 2.5 centimetres or less in diameter with either hand.	15
	(d) Cannot use a pen or pencil.	15
	(e) Cannot tie a bow in laces or string.	10
	(f) Cannot turn a sink tap or the control knobs on a cooker with one hand but can with the other.	6
	(g) Cannot pick up a coin which is 2.5 centimetres or less in diameter with one hand but can with the other.	6
	(h) No problem with manual dexterity.	0

Part 1 – Physical disabilities (continued)

Activity	Descriptor	Points
(8) Lifting and carrying by use of the upper body and arms (excluding all other activities in Part 1 of the Assessment)	(a) Cannot pick up a paperback book with either hand.	15
	(b) Cannot pick up and carry a 0.5 litre carton of milk with either hand.	15
	(c) Cannot pick up and pour from a full saucepan or kettle of 1.7 litre capacity with either hand.	15
	(d) Cannot pick up and carry a 2.5 kilogram bag of potatoes with either hand.	8
	(e) Cannot pick up and carry a 0.5 litre carton of milk with one hand, but can with the other.	6
	(f) Cannot pick up and carry a 2.5 kilogram bag of potatoes	0
(9) Reaching	(a) Cannot raise either arm as if to put something in the top pocket of a coat or jacket.	15
	(b) Cannot raise either arm to his or her head as if to put on a hat.	15
	(c) Cannot put either arm behind back as if to put on a coat or jacket.	15
	(d) Cannot raise either arm above his or her head as if to reach for something.	15
	(e) Cannot raise one arm to his or her head as if to put on a hat, but can with the other.	6
	(f) Cannot raise one arm above his or her head as if to reach for something but can with the other.	0
	(g) No problem with reaching.	0

Part 1 – Physical disabilities (continued)

Activity	Descriptor	Points
(10) Speech	(a) Cannot speak.	15
	(b) Speech cannot be understood by family or friends.	15
	(c) Speech cannot be understood by strangers.	15
	(d) Strangers have great difficulty understanding speech.	10
	(e) Strangers have some difficulty understanding speech.	8
	(f) No problems with speech.	0
(11) Hearing with a hearing aid or other aid if normally worn	(a) Cannot hear sounds at all.	15
	(b) Cannot hear well enough to follow a television programme with the volume turned up.	15
	(c) Cannot hear well enough to understand someone talking in a loud voice in a quiet room.	15
	(d) Cannot hear well enough to understand someone talking in a normal voice in a quiet room.	10
	(e) Cannot hear well enough to understand someone talking in a normal voice on a busy street.	8
	(f) No problem with hearing.	0

Part 1 – Physical disabilities (continued)

Activity	Descriptor	Points
(12) Vision in normal daylight or bright electric light with glasses or other aid to vision if such aid is normally worn	(a) Cannot tell light from dark.	15
	(b) Cannot see the shape of furniture in the room	15
	(c) Cannot see well enough to read 16 point print at a distance greater than 20 centimetres.	15
	(d) Cannot see well enough to recognise a friend across the room at a distance of at least five metres.	12
	(e) Cannot see well enough to recognise a friend across the road at a distance of at least 15 metres.	8
	(f) No problems with vision.	0
(13) Continence (other than enuresis)	(a) No voluntary control over bowels.	15
	(b) No voluntary control over bladder.	15
	(c) Loses control of bowels at least once a week.	15
	(d) Loses control of bowels at least once a month.	15
	(e) Loses control of bowels occasionally.	9
	(f) Loses control of bladder at least once a month.	3
	(g) Loses control of bladder occasionally.	0
	(h) No problem with continence.	0

Part 1 – Physical disabilities (continued)

Activity	Descriptor	Points
(14) Remaining conscious other than for normal periods of sleep	(a) Has an involuntary episode of lost or altered consciousness at least once a day.	15
	(b) Has an involuntary episode of lost or altered consciousness at least once a week.	15
	(c) Has an involuntary episode of lost or altered consciousness at least once a month.	15
	(d) Has had an involuntary episode of lost or altered consciousness at least twice in the six months before the day in respect to which it falls to be determined whether he or she is incapable of work for the purposes of entitlement to any benefit, allowance or advantage.	12
	(e) Has had an involuntary episode of lost or altered consciousness once in the six months before the day in respect to which it falls to be determined whether he or she is incapable of work for the purposes of entitlement to any benefit, allowance or advantage.	8
	(f) Has had an involuntary episode of lost or altered consciousness once in the three years before the day in respect to which it falls to be determined whether he or she is incapable of work for the purposes of entitlement to any benefit, allowance or advantage.	0
	(g) Has no problems with consciousness	0

Part 2. Mental illness and learning disabilities

Activity	Descriptor	Points
(15) Completion of tasks	(a) Cannot answer the telephone and reliably take a message.	2
	(b) Often sits for hours doing nothing.	2
	(c) Cannot concentrate to read a magazine article or follow a radio or television programme.	1
	(d) Cannot use a telephone book or other directory to find a number.	1
	(e) Mental condition prevents him or her from undertaking leisure activities previously enjoyed.	1
	(f) Overlooks or forgets the risk posed by domestic appliances or other common hazards due to poor concentration.	1
	(g) Agitation, confusion or forgetfulness has resulted in potentially dangerous accidents in the three months before the day in respect to which it falls to be determined whether he or she is incapable of work for the purposes of entitlement to any benefit, allowance or advantage.	1
	(h) Concentration can only be sustained by prompting.	1
(16) Daily living	(a) Needs encouragement to get up and dress.	2
	(b) Needs alcohol before midday.	2
	(c) Is frequently distressed at some time of the day due to fluctuation of mood.	1
	(d) Does not care about his or her appearance and living conditions.	1
	(e) Sleep problems interfere with his or her daytime activities.	1

Part 2. Mental illness and learning disabilities (continued)

Activity	Descriptor	Points
(17) Coping with pressure	**(a) Mental stress was a factor in making him or her stop work.**	2
	(b) Frequently feels scared or panicky for no obvious reason.	2
	(c) Avoids carrying out routine activities because he or she is convinced they will prove too tiring or stressful.	1
	(d) Is unable to cope with changes in daily routine.	1
	(e) Frequently finds there are so many things to do that he or she gives up because of fatigue, apathy or disinterest.	1
	(f) Is scared or anxious that work would bring back or worsen his or her illness.	1
(18) Interaction with other people.	**(a) Cannot look after himself or herself without help from others.**	2
	(b) Gets upset by ordinary events and it results in disruptive behavioural problems.	2
	(c) Mental problems impair ability to communicate with other people.	2
	(d) Gets irritated by things that would not have bothered him or her before he or she became ill.	1
	(e) Prefers to be left alone for six hours or more each day.	1
	(f) Is too frightened to go out alone.	1

Endnotes

[1] Schedule to Social Security (Incapacity for Work) (General) Regulations 1995

[2] Reg 25 (3) Social Security (Incapacity for Work) (General) Regulations 1995

[3] Reg 26 Social Security (Incapacity for Work) (General) Regulations 1995

Benefit rates

Weekly Benefit Rates 2007/2008

At the time of printing, the following benefit rates are current. These rates will be updated in April 2008 and will be published on the DWP website (www.dwp.gov.uk/advisers/ni17a/further_info/) and *Inclusion's* own homepage.

Means-tested Benefits

Income Support & income-based Jobseeker's Allowance

Personal allowances

Single person, aged 18-24	46.85
Single person, aged 25+	59.15
Lone parent, aged 18+	59.15
Couple	92.80
Dependent children[1]	47.45

Premiums

Carer	27.15
Disability, single	25.25
Disability, couple	36.00
Disabled Child[1]	46.69
Enhanced Disability, single person / lone parent	12.30
Enhanced Disability, couple	17.75
Enhanced Disability child[1]	18.76

Family[1]	16.43
Pensioner, single (JSA only)	59.90
Pensioner, couple	88.90
Severe Disability, per qualifying person	48.45

Housing Benefit & Council Tax Benefit

As for Income Support / income-based JSA or Pension Credit, except for:

Personal Allowances

Single person, under 18 (n/a for Council Tax Benefit)	46.85
Single person, aged 60-64	119.05
Single person, aged 65+	138.10

Lone parent, under 18 (n/a for CTB)	45.50
Couple, both under 18 (n/a for CTB)	68.65
Couple, one or both aged 65+	197.65
Couple, one or both aged 60-64	174.05

Premiums

Family, old lone parent rate	22.20
Family,	16.43
Family, baby rate	10.50

Working Tax Credit (annual rates)

Basic element	1,730
Couple / lone parent	1,700
30 hours element	705
Disability element	2,310
Severe disability element	980
50 + return to work, 16-29 hours	1,185
50 + return to work, 30+ hours	1,770

Childcare costs, one child (up to 80%)	Maximum:	175 (pw)
Childcare costs, two children (up to 80%)	Maximum:	300 (pw)

Child Tax Credit (annual rates)

Family element	545
Baby addition	545
Child element	1,845
Disabled child	2,440
Severely disabled child	980

Non means-tested Benefits

Attendance Allowance	lower rate	43.15
	higher rate	64.50

Bereavement Benefits[2]

Bereavement Allowance	87.30
Widowed Parent's Allowance	87.30
Widowed Parent's Allowance, child dependant	11.35[3]
Bereavement Payment (lump sum)	2,000

Carers Allowance

Carer's Allowance	48.65
Carer's Allowance, adult dependant	29.05
Carer's Allowance, child dependant	11.35[3]

Child Benefit

Only/eldest child	18.10
Other children	12.10

Disability Living Allowance

Care component	low rate	17.10
	Middle rate	43.15
	High rate	64.50
Mobility Component	lower rate	17.10
	Higher rate	45.00

Incapacity Benefit

Short term (under pension age)	lower rate	61.35
	higher rate	72.55
Child dependant (paid with higher rate)		11.35[3]
Short term (under pension age) adult dependant		37.90
Long term		81.35
Long term, age addition	lower rate (under 35)	8.55
	higher rate (35-44)	17.10
Long term, adult dependant		48.65
Long term, child dependant		11.35[3]
Long term inv. allowance	lower rate	5.50
	middle rate	11.00
	higher rate	17.10

Industrial Injuries Disablement Benefit

(Variable depending on % disablement)

Aged 18+	26.34 – 131.70
Jobseeker's Allowance (contribution based)	
Under 18	35.65
Aged 18-24	46.85
Aged 25+	59.15

Maternity Allowance

Standard rate	112.75
Adult Dependant	37.90

Severe Disablement Allowance

Severe Disablement Allowance		49.15
Age addition	lower rate (aged 50-59)	5.50
	middle rate (aged 40-49)	11.00
	higher rate (aged under 40)	17.10
Adult dependant		29.25
Child dependant		11.35[3]

Statutory Maternity, Paternity & Adoption Pay

	(standard rate)	112.75
Earnings Threshold		87.00

Statutory Sick Pay

Statutory Sick Pay	72.55
Earnings theshold	87.00

National Minimum Wage

	(per hour) From Oct '06
Aged 22+	£5.35
Aged 18-21 or in approved training	£4.45
Aged 16-18	£3.30

Endnotes

[1] If Child Tax Credit is not awarded. Otherwise paid via Child Tax Credit.

[2] Widow's Pension and Widowed Mother's Allowance paid at the same rates

[3] For claims made before 6th April 2004 and no Child Tax Credit awarded.

30 Abbreviations

AA	Attendance Allowance
ADF	Adviser Discretion Fund
BET	Basic Employability Training
CA	Carer's Allowance
CB	Child Benefit
CBEP	Child Benefit Extension Period
CV	Curriculum Vitae
CJSA	Contribution-based Jobseeker's Allowance
CTB	Council Tax Benefit
CTC	Child Tax Credit
DfES	Department for Education and Skills
DLA	Disability Living Allowance
DM	Decision Maker
DMG	Decision Maker's Guide
DWP	Department for Work and Pensions
EEA	European Economic Area
EC	European Community
EO	Employment Option
ETFO	Environment Task Force Option
ETO	Education and Training Opportunities
EU	European Union
EZ	Employment Zone
FE	Further Education
FTET	Full-time Education and Training
HB	Housing Benefit
HMRC	Her Majesty's Revenue and Customs
IAP	Intensive Activity Period
IB	Incapacity Benefit
IBJSA	Income-based Jobseeker's Allowance
IS	Income Support

IWC	In Work Credit
JMA	Jobseeker Mandatory Activity
JSA	Jobseeker's Allowance
LA	Local Authority
LFI	Learning Focused Interview
LPIWC	Lone Parent In Work Credit
LPWSP	Lone Parent Work Search Premium
LSC	Learning and Skills Council
LOT	Longer Occupational Training
MIP	Music Industry Provider
MIRO	Mortgage Interest Run On
MOL	Music Open Learning
MOLP	Musician's Open Learning Provider
ND25+	New Deal 25 Plus
ND50+	New Deal 50 Plus
NDDP	New Deal for Disabled People
NDLP	New Deal for Lone Parents
NDfM	New Deal for Musicians
NDP	New Deal for Partners
NDPA	New Deal personal adviser
NDYP	New Deal for Young People
NI	National Insurance
NVQ	National Vocational Qualification
Ofsted	Office for Standards in Education
p2w	progress2work
PC	Pension Credit
PCA	Personal Capability Assessment
SDA	Severe Disablement Allowance
SF	Social Fund
SMP	Statutory Maternity Pay
SSP	Statutory Sick Pay
SVQ	Scottish Vocational Qualification
TfW	Training for Work
TIC	Travel to Interview Scheme
UK	United Kingdom
VSO	Voluntary Sector Option
WBL	Work Based Learning
WBLA	Work Based Learning for Adults
WFI	Work Focused Interview
WTC	Working Tax Credit

Index